Economic Personalism

Property, Power and Justice for Every Person

Michael D. Greaney
and
Dawn K. Brohawn

Justice University Press

Center for Economic and Social Justice

Center for Economic and Social Justice
Arlington, Virginia, U.S.A.
Justice University Press

Published by Justice University Press, an imprint of the
Center for Economic and Social Justice
P. O. Box 40711, Washington, D.C. 20016 U.S.A.
(Tel) 703-243-5155 • (Fax) 703-243-5935
(Eml) publications@cesj.org • (Web) www.cesj.org

International Standard Book Number: 978-0-944997-13-0

Library of Congress Control Number: 2020946637

Cover design by Rowland L. Brohawn

Authors' Note, Some Definitions, and Acknowledgements

This book was written in response to a request to explain to the Catholic hierarchy, clergy, and scholars the fundamentals of economic personalism and how this relates to a conceptual framework called the "Just Third Way." The Just Third Way offers a fundamental alternative to the two prevailing socio-economic paradigms of capitalism and socialism/communism and their hybrids. We have therefore stressed broad concepts and historical developments over technical details and specific applications of principles.

While the book was being written, we realized that it could also serve to introduce the subject to the Catholic laity as well as to people of other faiths and philosophies. We have therefore tried to clarify specifically Catholic terms and concepts, especially those relating to the development of Catholic teaching in social and economic justice. Fortunately, there is common ground, since Catholic social teaching (like that of most faiths and philosophies) is based on the natural law as reflected in our human nature.

While this book has our names on the cover, it is the result of the collaborative work of many people over many years whose ideas have gone into the development of the Just Third Way of the interfaith Center for Economic and Social Justice (CESJ). Of particular note are Dr. Norman G. Kurland, president of CESJ and pioneer in the global development of the Just Third Way paradigm of socio-economics, Employee Stock Ownership Plans (ESOPs) and expanded capital ownership monetary and tax reforms, and Tomasz Pompowski, Strategic Communications Specialist, who is a former Vatican journalist and translator for Lech Wałęsa. Tom was a field producer for the documentary film *Nine Days That Changed the World* (2010) and gave us access to some of his research notes about Pope Saint John Paul II.

Although they are explained in the text, it is useful to define three key terms here to help orient the reader:

The Just Third Way. Within the economic context, a free market system based on principles of economic justice and the equal dignity, rights, and opportunity of each human person. All social institutions are structured to empower economically every person through the democratization of money and credit for new production, thereby providing universal access to direct ownership of future income-producing capital and protection of private property rights of all owners. This socio-economic paradigm offers a logical "third alternative" to the two predominant paradigms today — capitalism and social-ism/communism.

Personalism. A school of thought, or intellectual movement, which focuses on the reality of each person's unique dignity and promotes the fundamental human rights of each human person. Personalism also recognizes the social nature of human beings, who as members of groups create institutions to support each person's wellbeing and dignity. Personalism rejects the idea that the State or any form of society or collective creates rights; it posits that rights are inherent in each human being. Personalism seeks the empowerment and full development of every person, not only to realize one's own human potential and individual good, but also to be liberated and educated to work for the good of others and for the common good. It offers principles for restructuring social, political and economic institutions and laws toward that end.

Economic Personalism. An economic system centered on the dignity and economic empowerment of each person. It recognizes that life, dignity, and liberty require that each person have the power and independent means to support and sustain one's own life, dignity and liberty — i.e., through one's private property rights. Economic personalism aims to diffuse economic power structurally by democratizing access to capital ownership for each person.

As this book is meant to be merely an introduction to the Just Third Way of economic personalism, we have deliberately limited it to a broad treatment of basic principles, moral philosophy and general economic concepts. Because of that, some statements may come across as assertion, but giving detailed explanations here would have required a multi-volume work instead of a brief presentation. In-depth treatments of selected topics will be found in the materials listed in the Selected Bibliography and Resource Guide in the back of the book.

Throughout this book the goal has been analogous to that sought by Wesley Newcomb Hohfeld (1879-1918) with respect to jurisprudence in *Fundamental Legal Conceptions* (1919). That is, to isolate and identify basic concepts of Catholic social teaching, making it possible to define issues more precisely and develop solutions consistent with the principles of natural law and the Gospels.

Readers familiar with the work of CESJ will recognize much they have seen before. Two exceptions are Chapters 1 and 2, which were summarized from an upcoming book on the origins and development of social justice, and Chapter 3, based in part on material previously unavailable in English.

Note on the text: except where it is obvious from the context, the terms "man," "he," "his," and so on, refer to all human persons and are not restricted to adult human males.

Michael D. Greaney and Dawn K. Brohawn
Center for Economic and Social Justice

Table of Contents

Preface

Nearly five years before the Soviet Union officially dissolved, an historic meeting took place that escaped the world's notice and barely survived a last-minute cancellation. At the time even the participants in the meeting missed its full significance.

On February 9, 1987, representatives of President Ronald Reagan's Presidential Task Force on Project Economic Justice (PEJ), including founders of the interfaith Center for Economic and Social Justice who conceived the Task Force, had assembled at the Vatican with members of the Polish Solidarity Movement (*Solidarność*). They had been granted a private audience with His Holiness Pope John Paul II.

Headed by Norman G. Kurland, Deputy Chairman of the Task Force and President of CESJ, the delegation had traveled from the U.S. and Poland to present to His Holiness the bipartisan Task Force's report, *High Road to Economic Justice*. (This unanimous report was later delivered to President Reagan in a White House ceremony on August 3, 1987.)

The PEJ report offered a peaceful, justice-based strategy to counter the spread of Marxist-Leninism throughout Central America and the Caribbean region by promoting worker ownership through Employee Stock Ownership Plans (ESOPs). *Solidarność* members had translated into Polish the Project Economic Justice orientation book, *Every Worker an Owner*, and had distributed 40,000 copies throughout the country.

Earlier, when the delegation's U.S. contingent had arrived at the airport in Rome, they were told that their meeting with the pope had been canceled. The delegation had been "bumped" at the last minute by a head of state requesting a papal audience.

Upon receiving this disappointing news, Rabbi Herzel Kranz, head of an orthodox Jewish congregation in Silver Spring, Maryland and a key figure in the formation of the Presidential Task Force, sprang into action. He convinced the organizer of the papal audience, the Very Reverend Cassian Yuhaus, C.P. (former head of the Center for Applied Research in the Apostolate), to appeal to His Excellency then-Archbishop Achille Silvestrini to intercede.

Archbishop Silvestrini, the Vatican's Secretary of State for Public Affairs and a close friend of Fr. Cassian's, agreed to do what he could. The delegation was squeezed into the pope's busy schedule.

His Holiness warmly received the members of the delegation outside his private library and encouraged them in their work. He also
recommended that they collaborate with His Eminence Roger Cardinal Etchegaray, President of the Pontifical Council on Justice and
Peace, to educate Vatican scholars on the ideas contained in the Task
Force report.

Over the next several years, with now-Cardinal Silvestrini's support and Fr. Cassian's counsel, CESJ continued to build connections
within the Vatican with officials including Paul Cardinal Poupard,
head of the Pontifical Council on Culture. In 1991, CESJ organized a
conference in Rome for Vatican scholars on a socio-economic paradigm later called the "Just Third Way." Speakers focused on social
teachings of the Catholic Church, particularly the encyclicals of
Popes Leo XIII and Pius XI, which emphasized the importance of
widespread capital ownership.

Highlighted in the conference presentations were the definition
and principles of "Social Justice" as articulated by Pius XI, a sociolo-
gist who analyzed the moral relationship between the human person,
social institutions and the Common Good. (Pius XI's concepts of Social Justice had been at the heart of CESJ's founding in 1984, when
they were introduced by Reverend William Ferree, SM, Ph.D., a
world-recognized scholar in the social philosophy of Pius XI.)

The conference also focused on the three principles of "Economic
Justice" as defined by corporate finance lawyer and expanded ownership economist Louis O. Kelso and his co-author, Aristotelian-Thomist philosopher Mortimer J. Adler. Their systematized understanding of Economic Justice, also adopted by CESJ, addressed the moral
omissions in both Capitalism and Socialism. Incorporated within
Kelso's theory of "binary economics," these principles informed the
financial technologies and institutional reforms Kelso invented (and
CESJ later refined). These enable every citizen, even those lacking
savings to invest, to purchase a personal stake of capital assets.

Following the Rome conference, CESJ's delegation was granted a second audience with Pope John Paul II in which His Holiness was presented with a special edition of *Every Worker an Owner*. The papal audience and conference led to further progress. CESJ published several
books on the principles and applications for creating a Culture of Life,
Liberty and Justice, with economic independence for every person.

CESJ's "pro-life economic agenda" provides the reasons and reforms for extending to every member of society full access to the Common Good, including the monetary system. With access through the
commercial and central banking system to newly created asset-

backed money and insured capital credit, every person every year, from birth to death, would gain the means to purchase shares of new and transferred capital.

The two audiences with Pope John Paul II symbolized a confluence of revolutionary ideas developed over the centuries. Principles and theories of social and economic justice, universal human rights, non-violent social change, and free market economics could be practically applied. This was now possible thanks to a new understanding of money and credit as tools for financing sustainable and *broadly owned* economic growth in a globalized and technology-driven world.

This synthesis of social, economic, and political thought would coalesce as a "Just Third Way" transcending systems of individualism and collectivism that concentrate power in a private *élite* or in the State. Not fully appreciated by CESJ until recently was Pope John Paul II's own profound contributions to the philosophical orientation known as "Personalism."

Today His Holiness Pope Francis faces deep divisions within the Church, while external threats are driving apart people, nations and the world. The global community faces a deadly pandemic with no end in sight, impending economic collapse, rising trade wars and military tensions, dissolution of alliances, devastating climate change, and a growing gap in wealth, power and opportunity between the richest 1% and 99% of the world's citizens.

The poorest of the poor, now facing sheer starvation, have been virtually forgotten by politicians, academia, the media and the general public. Ultra-nationalist, anti-immigrant, and racist sentiments are winning over, with alarming rapidity, the hearts and minds of ordinary citizens. At the opposite end of the ideological spectrum, self-styled "progressives" and "democratic socialists" are calling upon the State to redistribute income and wealth.

This book, *Economic Personalism: Property, Power and Justice for Every Person*, explores a new path for the future. By understanding the moral basis of John Paul II's "Personalism" and the ideas of other "personalist" and "post-scarcity" thinkers, we can identify the elements of a new paradigm for overcoming humanity's greatest challenges. With new assumptions, we can conceive a new economy based on the dignity, development and empowerment of every human person, within a just social order and life-enhancing environment.

As explained in *Economic Personalism*, every member of society — including the poorest of the poor, the unemployed, and those unable to engage in economic work — can become a fully empowered producer and consumer in the economy. Our basic institutions can be restructured to provide truly equal economic opportunity through equal access to the means to become an owner of future productive capital, *without having to redistribute anyone's existing wealth.*

This new possibility starts with a re-examination of justice, property, and the role of money and credit as "social tools." As Pope Francis has stated, we must say "No" to the *worship* of money and the material goods of this world. Only when such things as the State, corporations and money are returned to their proper role as humanity's servants — not its masters — can we dismantle the systemic barriers that divide people instead of uniting them.

With the proper functioning of money within a more just economic system, advanced technologies of all kinds could free every person from dehumanizing toil. Unfettered by the daily struggle for subsistence and survival, each of us would be free to develop our highest human potential and pursue our highest spiritual needs. Each of us could own and not be owned.

Economic Personalism posits that there are universal moral values and principled yet effective means for reforming human institutions to liberate and empower every human person. It affirms John Paul II's observation that the economic system and society as a whole benefit when the rights, values, and dignity of each person are respected.

When we have conquered systemic poverty, we can all become, as global design scientist R. Buckminster Fuller put it: "Architects of the future, not its victims." We will have the means to become better stewards of Nature, prospering in harmony with the natural world rather than destroying it. The Personalist approach to building a just global economy will also eliminate the economic causes of war, bringing global unity in support of eliminating weapons of mass destruction.

Ultimately, *Economic Personalism* is a tribute to the vision of John Paul II and other pioneering thinkers who have advanced the dignity and empowerment of every person as the basis for an effective democratic order, a good society, and the beloved community.

As a guide for Pope Francis and other world leaders, the idea of Economic Personalism as a "Just Third Way" above and beyond Capitalism and Socialism has the potential to bring about a new era of justice, ownership, freedom and peace for all people throughout the world.

1
The Question of the Person

Confronted today by growing conflict and inequality between people and nations around the globe, no one can ignore any longer the universal question that will shape the future for generations to come: What is the place of the human person — each of us — in society? This question is not academic, nor is it simple. It raises issues of human dignity, freedom, responsibility, and power — and who and what is entitled to those things. Must we accept the *status quo,* a system that fosters conflict, inequality, and injustice? Or can and should the social order at all levels be structured to operate justly for the good of every person everywhere, without the disadvantage of anyone anywhere?

To answer the original question, and whether such justice-based systemic reform is possible, we can look to the related concepts of "Personalism" and "Solidarity." To define what we mean by these terms, we begin with the thought of Pope Saint John Paul II (Karol Józef Wojtyła, 1920-2005, elected 1978[1]).

In February 1961, while still Auxiliary Bishop of Kraków, Wojtyła startled the intellectual community with his paper, "Personalizm Tomistyczny" ("Thomistic Personalism"), defining personalism as any school of thought, or any intellectual movement, that focuses on the reality of the human person and each person's unique dignity.[2] In the short article presenting personalism as an alternative, he countered ideologies that shift dignity and power away from the human person.

Suggesting that some later interpretations of the documents were not consistent with the original intent, during the Second Vatican Council (1962-1965), Wojtyła contributed to *Dignitatis Humanae* ("Decree on Religious Freedom") and *Gaudium et Spes* ("Pastoral Constitution on the Church in the Modern World").[3]

In Wojtyła's thought, the concept of solidarity holds an important place. As he would later state — putting the word in quotes — solidarity is a "virtue," the habit of doing good, but not in the same sense

---

[1] In general, we will use his given name in this book to stress the fact that John Paul II developed his principles before his election.
[2] Karol Wojtyła, "Personaolizm Tomistyczny," *Znak* 13 (1961): 664-675.
[3] Wojtyła and the other Polish bishops submitted a draft for *Gaudium et Spes* which, while influential, was not adopted as the base text.

as, for example, justice and charity. In his encyclical issued as pope
on the twentieth anniversary of *Populorum Progressio* he explained
that solidarity —

> . . . is above all a question of interdependence, sensed as a system de-
> termining relationships in the contemporary world, in its economic,
> cultural, political and religious elements, and accepted as a moral cat-
> egory. When interdependence becomes recognized in this way, the cor-
> relative response as a moral and social attitude, as a "virtue," is soli-
> darity.[4]

Specifically, solidarity, a characteristic of groups *per se*, is a principle that fulfills and completes that general justice which permeates
all virtue, a sort of "general social charity."[5] It is not a particular virtue[6] (a virtue that is defined by a specific "act" directed at a specific
"object"), nor does it exclude non-Christians.[7]

In the context of Wojtyła's Thomistic personalism, then, solidarity
describes an awareness of rights and duties within a particular group
that define how sovereign individuals relate as persons to one another and to the group as a whole. All people as members of a group
have solidarity when they have that awareness and are able to participate fully as members of that group.

Solidarity in Wojtyła's thought is an essential prerequisite for social justice, for (as we will see) only members of groups can carry out
acts of social justice. By this means cooperation is achieved, not by
absorbing people into the group or collective, but by mutual interaction and give-and-take in exercising rights and attaining the common
goals and aspirations of the group.[8]

---

[4] *Solicitudo Rei Socialis*, § 38.

[5] Solidarity appears to relate to social charity as legal justice relates to social justice,
viz, a general virtue as it relates to a particular virtue.

[6] A general virtue, unlike a particular virtue, does not have a defined, "particular" act
or a direct object.

[7] Solidarity is a virtue Christians necessarily have, not one that is exclusive to Christians: "Solidarity is undoubtedly a Christian virtue. In what has been said so far it
has been possible to identify many points of contact between solidarity and charity,
which is the distinguishing mark of Christ's disciples." *Ibid.*, § 40.

[8] Solidarism as conceived by Wojtyła is in sharp contrast to that of, *e.g.*, the sociolo-
gist David Émile Durkheim (1858-1917). Durkheim, whose conception of God was a
"divinized society" (Fulton J. Sheen, *Religion Without God*. New York: Garden City
Books, 1954, 54), held that only the collective has rights. Individual ethics are merely
expedient and necessarily give way before the demands of social ethics. As Joseph Al-
ois Schumpeter (1883-1950) put it, for Durkheim, "religion is the group's worship of
itself." (Joseph A. Schumpeter, *History of Economic Analysis*. New York: Oxford University Press, 1954, 794.)

A common mistake today is to assume that social rights and virtues are rights and virtues that society or humanity as a whole has by nature. This is impossible, as "society" and "humanity" are abstractions, things created by human persons. Things have only such rights as human beings delegate to them. A social right or virtue is a right or virtue that human persons have with regard to society, not that society has with regard to persons.[9]

Together, Wojtyła's concepts of solidarity and Thomistic personalism provide more than an esoteric academic discussion, but a practical means for applying the principles of Catholic social teaching to many of today's otherwise overwhelming problems. Solidarity motivates our care for the common good. Personalism focuses our actions on promoting the dignity of every human being and on how each person can relate fully to society and to the common good. Combined, the two concepts offer a holistic paradigm for problem solving that puts even the most monumental tasks within the reach of every person acting in free association with others.

Today, many people throughout the world are forced to serve the State or a political or economic *élite* that controls the social tool of the State. This puts the most basic human needs, including subsistence and security, under the control of some who wield the State's monopoly over coercion. Because of the way institutions and laws have been structured, the *élite* are able to monopolize power and benefit themselves at the expense of others.

Ultimately, every issue in religious, political, or family life concerns human dignity. What does it mean to be a person? Who should have power and thus control over the life and even the soul of the human person? Are human beings mere things to be owned by others, the State or a political or economic *élite*? Or are human beings born with equal worth and inalienable rights, and thus meant to have the power and means to pursue their own higher ends or destinies?

To answer these questions we must first ask with the Psalmist, "What is man, that thou art mindful of him?"[10] The answer might surprise many people, and upset many preconceptions about ourselves, our fellow human beings, and our place in the world.

---

[9] Cf. the distinction between a right *in personam*, a right a human person has in regard to himself, and a right *in rem*, a right a human person has in regard to a thing. Wesley Newcomb Hohfeld, *Fundamental Legal Conceptions.* New Haven, Connecticut: Yale University Press, 1946, 65-114.

[10] Psalms 8:5.

Faith and Reason

Man, as Aristotle noted in the *Politics*, is the rational animal.[11] Anything that shifts the human person away from reason as the foundation of a faith or a philosophy contradicts essential human nature, that is, what it means to be human.

Ralph Michael McInerny (1929-2010), professor of philosophy at the University of Notre Dame, once commented that fideism is the single greatest danger to Catholicism in the world today.[12] Fideism is the idea that truth is determined by what one believes, rather than what can be proved by reason or that is consistent with reason and thus conforms to natural law. Natural law is defined here as the universal code of human behavior, while human understanding of truth is that which conforms to reality, reality being something independent of the human mind that perceives it.[13]

Behind fideism is the idea that truth as truth is no longer an ultimate goal or good. As with people who believe in a flat Earth, for example, what is objectively true becomes of lesser importance, in extreme cases even irrelevant compared to what they want to believe. Their adherence to personal opinion or blind, uncomprehending acceptance of dogma, persists even after they are presented with evidence to the contrary.

Often what matters are the pronouncements of whatever authority someone accepts, usually interpreted to fit some predetermined position. Faith in authority becomes more important than empirical validity or logical consistency.

Disagreements become settled not on the basis of fact or of logical argument, but by whoever's faith is stronger or (more accurately) whose opinion can be expressed most forcefully or becomes most popular. As legal scholar Heinrich Albert Rommen (1897-1967) noted, by abandoning reason and basing beliefs solely on faith, what follows is moral positivism — the belief that right and wrong depend only on

---

[11] *Politics*, 1252a.

[12] Ralph M. McInerny, *Miracles: A Catholic View*. Huntington, Indiana: Our Sunday Visitor, 1986, 22.

[13] Mortimer J. Adler, *Truth in Religion: The Plurality of Religions and the Unity of Truth*. New York: Macmillan Publishing Company, 1990, 21-22. Cf. J.M. Bocheński, *The Methods of Contemporary Thought*. New York: Harper & Row, Publishers, 1968, 3-5, 6.

the will of some authority, not objective reality or truth — leading almost inevitably to nihilism, the belief that life is meaningless.[14]

Moral positivism and nihilism lead to contempt for other people, then of everything except one's self, and finally even of one's self. That is why, as Gilbert Keith Chesterton (1874-1936) remarked, there is so little real argument these days, and so much sneering.[15]

By shifting the determination of truth and goodness from what can be observed of human nature, to some human authority or to an idealized abstraction of humanity, fideism directly undermines the dignity of every child, woman, and man. Dignity, which relates to all human needs (including security and survival), is the "quality or state of being worthy, honored, or esteemed."[16]

Every single human being, simply because he is a human being and thus a person, is "worthy, honored, or esteemed." By calling fundamental truths into question, fideism undermines or even nullifies the power every person needs to control his own life. By attacking truth, faith without reason is thus not only a serious threat to the Catholic Church as McInerny claimed, but to any and all natural religions and philosophies throughout the world.

One of the most serious problems associated with fideism is the tendency to confuse conclusions and beliefs based on religious faith, with those derived from scientific enquiry. Both religious truth and scientific truth are true, but some believers are tempted to impose beliefs based on faith on others who do not accept their particular faith.

Forcing religious beliefs on others violates free will and offends against human dignity. It also fails to take into account that while scientific truth and religious truth are both true, they are, nevertheless, different aspects of the truth as a universal and absolute principle, and are proved or accepted in different ways. As the Great Books philosopher Mortimer Jerome Adler (1901-2001) commented in a discussion of knowledge and opinion,

> Religious belief or faith would lose all its efficacy if it were reduced to mere opinion. But the grounds on which it makes such a claim are so utterly different from the criteria we have employed to divide genuine knowledge from mere opinion that it is impossible within the scope of

---

[14] Heinrich A. Rommen, *The Natural Law: A Study in Legal and Social History and Philosophy*. Indianapolis, Indiana: Liberty Fund, Inc., 1998, 51-52.
[15] G.K. Chesterton, *Saint Thomas Aquinas: The "Dumb Ox"*. New York: Image Books, 1956, 126.
[16] "Dignity," Meriam-Webster Dictionary.

this discussion to put religious faith or belief into the picture we now have before us.[17]

Attempting to impose religious beliefs or lack thereof on others in the form of a political, social, or economic philosophy (or anything else) is not merely contrary to reason and therefore to nature. It is detrimental to the common good, that vast network of institutions (social habits) within which people realize their personal goods.[18]

That there is a Creator, and that the Nature of that Creator consists of absolute good, can according to Catholic belief be proved by human reason, but nothing more.[19] Anything else is based on faith that, while it cannot contradict reason, also cannot be proved empirically; it is necessarily an abstraction.

Abstractions are created by human beings and have no existence apart from the human mind. Thus, especially these days when moral relativism has attained the status of dogma, it is essential to restore a philosophy that is not centered on a subjective abstraction, but on objective reality. What is needed is personalism, a way of thinking based on the actuality of the human person created by God.

Consequently, what has been called the "Just Third Way" does not force people to conform to idealized and presumably perfect abstractions imposed by whomever happens to have enough power to control the lives of others. Rather, people are guided by their admittedly inadequate and imperfect understanding of the absolute values of ultimate reality reached through reason and observation. In this way, might does not make right; rather, we all grow and prosper when each and every person is able to relate to each other, society, and the common good as a whole in conformity with universal values, such as truth, beauty, love, and justice.

---

[17] Mortimer J. Adler, *Ten Philosophical Mistakes: Basic Errors in Modern Thought — How They Came About, Their Consequences, and How to Avoid Them.* New York: Macmillan Publishing Company, 1985, 105-106.
[18] Rev. William J. Ferree, S.M., Ph.D., *Introduction to Social Justice.* New York: Paulist Press, 1948, 23-30. Józef Maria Bocheński, O.P., of the Kraków Circle Thomists, construed the common good as a vast network of interdependent "states of being." Bocheński, *The Methods of Contemporary Thought, op. cit.,* 2-3. Cf. Alexis de Tocqueville, "Principal Causes Which Render Religion Powerful in America," *Democracy in America,* I.xvii.
[19] *Summa Theologica,* Ia, q. 1, aa. 7-8; First Vatican Council, Canon 2.1; The Oath Against Modernism; *Humani Generis,* § 2. See also Adler, *Truth in Religion, op. cit.*

The Reasonable Alternative

The question then becomes which principles best meet the need of each human person to pursue absolute values of Truth, Beauty, Love and Justice, and can therefore legitimately claim to be personalist.[20] As such principles are discerned by observation and reason, they must, of course, be based on or consistent with reason.

In this context a principle is a fundamental truth or proposition based on reason[21] that serves as the foundation for a system of belief or behavior. Principles, because they do not have a defined act or direct object on which to act, correspond to Aristotle's concept of general or legal justice.[22] They infuse and guide the exercise of all particular virtues, *i.e.*, those that do have defined acts and directed objects, but like solidarity and personalism are not themselves particular virtues.

It is an obvious truth that many people do not have the time or the expertise to reason every matter out for themselves and so rely on faith for their notions of good and evil. That, however, does not in any way change the fact that — again, according to Catholic belief — knowledge of God's existence and of the natural law can be known by human reason.

"Person" signifies "that which has rights." The personalist principle — respect for the dignity of every human being — must therefore guide the respect for the natural rights of each person, especially life, liberty, and access to the rights of private property. No system can be considered personalist that assumes rights come from any form of society (whether the whole of humanity, a special class of persons, or a single individual in an official capacity) or that God grants any rights directly to any form of society.

Finally, we must reject the idea that good and evil are purely matters of opinion or arbitrary religious beliefs. The potential to acquire and develop moral absolutes is inherent in the human condition. While we as imperfect human beings can never develop these absolutes perfectly, we can attain a better understanding of them by growing in virtue through exercising rights, that is, by pursuing justice. The question is how best to do this.

---

[20] The Catholic Church has selected Aristotelian-Thomism as interpreted by competent authority, but that does not necessarily preclude other philosophies from also being personalist.

[21] This is true even for purely faith-based principles, for they may not contradict reason. Hence *lex ratio*, "law is reason." Rommen, *The Natural Law, op. cit.*, 159-160.

[22] *Ethics*, 1129b25-1130a13.

Deciding which particular philosophy best meets the needs of actual people and conforms to essential human nature (that is, to truth), is paradoxically neither as difficult nor as easy as it sounds. It requires simply that we follow the dictum, "To thine own self be true."[23]

Yet being true to one's self — that is, conforming to one's human nature — and becoming more fully human in the process by acquiring and developing virtue ("human-ness"), if done at all, is the work of a lifetime and the hardest path to follow. It is all the more difficult in the modern world because so many people are powerless and have been alienated from the social order. This runs counter to a fundamental aspect of human nature. As Aristotle noted, in addition to being the animal that reasons, "man is by nature a political animal."[24]

The Political Animal

To explain, human beings are neither isolated individuals nor undifferentiated members of a collective. We are persons who by nature associate with one another in a consciously structured environment called the *pólis*, hence *political*.

While the *pólis* can be structured to encourage either virtue or vice, it is neither virtuous nor vicious in and of itself. We therefore speak of the social environment as being made up of structures of virtue or structures of vice or sin. Society may encourage us one way or another, but which way we go is ultimately our personal and joint responsibility, as is the structuring of the *pólis* itself.

It is important to realize that human beings are not only rational and political, but tool makers and users. There is, of course, also the irrational and emotional side of human beings, but since we are discussing personalism and the primacy of reason over irrationality, we will ignore it for the sake of the argument.

Consistent with human nature, then, we consciously structure and maintain our environment in both its physical and its social aspects to provide the opportunity and means to secure our wellbeing. Our physical environment, including the natural world around us, also consists of infrastructure, houses, factories, stores, roads, dams, bridges, and so on, that we possess individually or in association with others.

---

[23] *Hamlet*, Act I, Scene 3.
[24] *Politics*, 1253a.

Our social environment consists of a vast network of invisible structures comprising the common good that each person as such is supposed to possess in its entirety. This network includes laws, customs, traditions, and other institutions ("social habits"), and social tools such as money and credit, tax systems, even language and the State.

Both the physical and the social environment are tools by means of which the human person carries on the process of living. The process of living consists not only of providing for one's (and one's family's) survival and security, but furthermore by becoming virtuous, thereby becoming more fully human.

It is by means of these social tools that each person as a political animal satisfies not only his individual wants and needs, but his social wants and needs (*i.e.*, domestic and civil interpersonal relationships). Preferably this is done in a way that also assists each person in becoming virtuous, that is, more fully human.

In satisfying individual wants and needs within a social framework there must also be no harm done to others or to the common good, and ideally what is done should indirectly benefit the whole of society. To participate fully in society, then, each person must have full access to those invisible structures of the common good, the tools for living in society.

Therein lies what may very well be the greatest immediate problem of the modern age. It underlies all social problems that prevent or inhibit each person developing more fully as a human being.

That problem is the inability of many people to satisfy their individual material wants and needs in a way that respects their own dignity, does not offend or harm the dignity of others, and benefits society, or at least does no harm. This is because most people have been stripped of power, and thus of control over their own lives.

The Age of Revolution

To oversimplify somewhat, three revolutions have led to the alienation of most people from the institutions of the common good by stripping them of power. The first two did this almost inadvertently by limiting access to social and technological tools, while the third did it by the nature of the change itself. These were,

- **The Financial Revolution,** the reinvention of commercial banking in the fourteenth century and the invention of central banking in the late seventeenth century,

- **The Industrial Revolution,** the invention of machinery that could out-produce human labor at an exponential rate, and
- **The Political Revolution,** widespread upheavals sparked in reaction to existing conditions and social orders that denied the dignity, rights and powers of every person, and which evolved into three distinct socio-economic philosophies.

At more or less the same time, and combining with the three revolutions, three worldviews gained a new lease on life and began to spread. It is important to note that only the third of these world views is based on both the individual and social aspects of the human person. They were,

- **Individualism.** Only an *élite*, a special or favored class of persons, has effective rights and thus dignity, and the ability to realize its full humanity,
- **Collectivism.** Only humanity as a whole has rights by nature and thus dignity applies to the abstraction of the collective,[25] and
- **Personalism.**[26] Every human person has rights by nature, is of equal dignity, and is fully human; thus, any school of thought, or any intellectual movement that focuses on the reality of the human person and each person's unique dignity.[27]

Not by coincidence, three political philosophies developed out of and correspond to three views about human beings. All three were called liberal democracy,[28] meaning government "of the people, by the people, and for the people,"[29] yet what each meant by "people" and "person" differed significantly from the other two.[30] They were,

---

[25] See Fulton J. Sheen, *God and Intelligence in Modern Philosophy* (1925) and *Religion Without God* (1927).

[26] The earliest use of the term "personalism" appears to have been by Friedrich Daniel Ernst Schleiermacher (1768-1834) in *Über die Religion* (1799).

[27] Thomas D. Williams, L.C., "What is Thomistic Personalism?" *Alpha Omega*, Vol. VII, No. 2, 2004, 164.

[28] This discussion covers only political liberalism, not religious liberalism. Religious liberalism is the idea that all religions are equally true, which also means they are all equally false. The analysis of political liberalism is based on that of George H. Sabine, *A History of Political Theory, Third Edition*. New York: Holt, Rinehart and Winston, 1961, 669-753.

[29] As Sabine defined it, liberalism is "a fundamental postulate about the nature of value, *viz.*, that all value inheres ultimately in the satisfactions and the realizations of human personality." *Ibid.*, 670.

[30] See Joseph Ratzinger, *Europe: Today and Tomorrow*. San Francisco, California: Ignatius Press, 2004; Joseph Ratzinger and Marcello Pera, *Without Roots: The West, Relativism, Christianity, Islam*. New York: Basic Books, 2006.

- **English Liberal Democracy.** An élite is sovereign and has power,
- **French or European Liberal Democracy.** The abstraction of the collective, not every human person, is sovereign and has power, and
- **American Liberal Democracy.** Every human person is sovereign, and thus political power is spread out among citizens.[31]

It is outside the scope of this discussion, but it is useful to know that the theology the Catholic Church calls by the misleading name of "modernism" is common to both individualism and collectivism. Modernism shifts focus away from God, the uncreated ultimate reality, to an abstraction created by human beings that has no existence apart from the human mind.

Finally, there are three systems of political economy that arose, corresponding to these political philosophies. These are,

- **Capitalism.** Allows for concentrated private capital ownership and thus concentrated power; thus, only a private sector *élite* has access to the opportunity and means to be fully productive,
- **Socialism.** Abolishes private capital ownership and thus personal power; only the collective has access to the opportunity and means to be fully productive.
- **Economic Personalism.** Spreads private capital ownership, and thus power; it holds that every person is entitled to equal opportunity and access to the means to be fully productive and empowered,[32]

---

[31] Contradicted by the institution of chattel slavery.

[32] It should be noted the term "economic personalism" has at least three other meanings in addition to the one given here, of which their respective adherents claim are consistent with the personalism of John Paul II. These correspond to capitalism, socialism, and the Servile or Welfare State, and are thus not fully consistent with the essential respect for human dignity that characterizes the personalism of John Paul II. The capitalist position can be found in Gregory M.A. Gronbacher, *Economic Personalism: A New Paradigm for a Humane Economy* (Grand Rapids, Michigan: Acton Institute, 1998). The socialist position is seen in Daniel Rush Finn, "The Economic Personalism of John Paul II: Neither Right Nor Left" (*Journal of Markets and Morality* 2 (1999) 74-87). The Servile/Welfare State position is seen in Richard J. Coronado, "*Centesimus Annus* and Key Elements of John Paul II's Political Economy," Benedictine College (https://www.benedictine.edu/academics/departments/economics/centesimus-annus-and-key-elements-john-paul-iis-political-economy, accessed August 22, 2019).

The matrix below outlines the relationship between these three conceptual paradigms, political philosophies, and systems of political economy:

Individualism	Collectivism	Personalism
English Liberal Democracy	European Liberal Democracy	American Liberal Democracy
Capitalism	Socialism	Economic Personalism

All of these arose in response to fundamental changes in the institutions of the common good brought about by the three revolutions noted above, the order of which is no coincidence.

As an important advance in the institutions of the common good, the Financial Revolution enabled people to finance new capital formation without first reducing consumption and accumulating money savings.[33] This provided the opportunity and means to advance technologically through new forms of productive capital, such as the steam engine and the power loom.

Most people, however, had no significant savings or accumulated wealth to collateralize[34] money creation. They were thereby cut off from access to credit extended through the commercial/mercantile and central banking systems. This virtually ensured that ownership of the new capital instruments would be concentrated, with most people restricted to selling their labor to generate income.[35]

From being independent small owners and laborers able to generate sufficient income for themselves and their dependents, large numbers of people were forced into a condition of dependency on

---

[33] This had always been possible, but it had previously been based exclusively on the creditworthiness of an individual or small group. What commercial/mercantile banking backed up by a central bank did was make "pure credit" part of the overall financial system. "Pure credit" is not a loan of existing savings but of money created based on the feasibility of the productive project for which financing is sought. Thus, in theory, anyone could participate in money creation for a capital project that was expected to repay its financing.

[34] A pledge of assets by the borrower to secure the lender against loss in the event of a default.

[35] Hilaire Belloc, *The Servile State*. Indianapolis, Indiana: Liberty Fund, Inc., 1977, 100-101.

private employers.[36] Toward the end of the nineteenth century the financial obligations became too great for the private sector, and the State began taking over much of the burden.[37]

By the middle of the twentieth century, the Welfare or Servile State (although not in the form Joseph Hilaire Pierre René Belloc, 1870-1953, anticipated) had in many instances displaced ownership of both labor and capital as the primary source of income for many people. As predicted,[38] the cost of sustaining the social welfare system soon became too great for the tax base of virtually any country to sustain,[39] even with massive government debt and currency manipulation.[40]

At the dawn of the twenty-first century, the global financial system was overburdened with non-productive government debt. Widespread national bankruptcies were avoided only by massive debt rescheduling and counterproductive austerity measures. Even so, these did not address the underlying problem: lack of opportunity and means to be productive on the part of a large number of people and even entire nations.[41]

The Financial and Industrial Revolutions introduced fundamental changes at a previously unheard-of rate into a society still under stress as a result of the emergence of Europe from the Middle Ages. Based on a version of liberal democracy directly at odds with that of the American Revolution, the French Revolution undertook to address the problems of society by destroying institutions instead of reforming them.

Reform efforts following the French Revolution attempted either to restore the old order, or to improve on or extend the revolutionary model. The few exceptions, such as that of Pope Pius VII (Luigi Barnabà Chiaramonte, 1742-1823, elected 1800) that endeavored to implement a measure of American liberal democracy in the Papal States, were generally unsuccessful.

---

[36] Hilaire Belloc, *An Essay on the Restoration of Property.* New York: Sheed and Ward, 1936, 37-59.
[37] Goetz A. Briefs, *The Proletariat: A Challenge to Western Civilization.* New York: McGraw-Hill Book Company, 1937, 177-179.
[38] *Ibid.,* 253-256.
[39] "Since the [First World] War, featuring as one of its manifold consequences, this burden has grown beyond anything ever dreamed of." (*Ibid.,* 256.)
[40] Harold G. Moulton, *The Recovery Problem in the United States.* Washington, DC: The Brookings Institution, 1936, 36-49.
[41] The hostility of governments to private sector productive activity is a mantra of capitalists the world over, but there is a great deal of truth in it.

Conditions were ripe for even more revolutionary change, and the emerging socialist movement seized the opportunity. Although the term socialism did not appear until the early 1830s, what was originally called "the Democratic Religion," "New Christianity," "Neo-Catholicism," and a variety of other labels described a multitude of systems all based on the theory of socialism. That is, sovereignty resides in some form of the collective, an abstraction, not in the actuality of flesh and blood individual persons.

This led naturally to the first principle of socialism: that the whole of society, construed as exclusively economic in nature, should be devoted to material improvement, with special emphasis on uplifting the poor, as the sole end of life.[42] Meeting material wants and needs, not becoming more fully human, became the purpose of existence.

Need, not exchange or reciprocity, redefined justice, disregarding the classical meaning of that virtue. Consequently, all forms of socialism end up turning most people into permanent dependents. Such dependency hinders most people from moving beyond their basic survival and security needs, and thus from becoming more fully human.

In contrast, the Catholic Church has always regarded the corporal works of mercy[43] as coming under charity, not justice. As far as the Church is concerned, the ultimate meaning and purpose of life goes beyond simply meeting one's material wants and needs.

Rather, satisfying one's material wants and needs is only one essential step on the way to becoming more fully human and thus preparing one's self for a final end (one's ultimate purpose in life), however that might be understood in a particular faith or philosophy. The specific means by which the corporal works of mercy are carried out is a matter of expedience and prudence,[44] but they must not be coerced, as the socialists demand, or they cease to be works of mercy and cannot be considered charitable.

We see this reflected in Maslow's "Hierarchy of Human Needs," which puts material needs at the base of the pyramid at the lowest but most urgent level, and self-actualization at the top. In addition we would either say that self-actualization to fulfill one's human potential includes serving God and working with others to perfect the

---

[42] "Saint-Simon," *Encyclopedia Britannica*, 19: 14th Edition, 1956, Print.
[43] Feeding the hungry, giving drink to the thirsty, sheltering the homeless, visiting the sick, visiting prisoners, burying the dead, and giving alms to the poor.
[44] That is, the corporal works of mercy must be carried out in a manner suitable to the case or situation (expedient) and consistent with reason and good judgment (prudent).

common good and civilization, or would add those to another level above self-actualization:

Expansion of Maslow's Hierarchy

The Theory of Certitude

As promoted by Robert Owen (1771-1858), Claude-Henri de Rouvroy, comte de Saint-Simon (1760-1825), François-Marie-Charles Fourier (1772-1837), and others, socialism sought to abolish traditional concepts of private property, marriage and family, and religion. In their place would be new institutions that might go by the same name and even have the same outward form as the old institutions (Saint-Simon, for instance, called his system, "the New Christianity"), but the substance would be completely different.

From the Catholic point of view, the worst of the new systems was Neo-Catholicism as promoted by Hugues-Félicité-Robert de Lamennais (1782-1854).[45] De Lamennais, unquestionably a genius, based his system of Christian socialism on a far more rigorous intellectual foundation than virtually all the others. His "theory of certitude" contained errors of such subtlety that many otherwise orthodox Catholics accept them even today, despite continued efforts by the Church to eradicate the errors.

Similar to the spirituality of the Medieval Fraticelli based in part on the condemned writings of Blessed Joachim of Flora (*cir.* 1132-1202)[46] and the nominalism of the sect's philosopher, William of

---

[45] De Lamennais did not develop Neo-Catholicism, but radically altered the work of others when he became the movement's acknowledged leader.

[46] Joachim's writings were condemned, but he is considered a beatus due to the fact that he submitted all his writings to the judgment of the Church. Edmund Garrett

Ockham (*cir.* 1287- *cir.* 1349),[47] de Lamennais's theory of certitude was a kind of *sensus communis* — a focus on the common good to the exclusion of individual good. It appealed to the universal testimony of the human race by faith instead of examining empirical evidence or making a logical argument to discern or evaluate religious truth.[48]

A further problem was that de Lamennais assumed that the abstractions he created in his own mind were more real than what could be demonstrated empirically or proven logically. Something was true because he believed it; he did not believe it because it was shown to be true.

De Lamennais therefore dismissed individual reason. He claimed truths such as knowledge of the existence of God and of the natural law reside only in the general reason as the result of direct revelation from God. According to de Lamennais, this requires a central religious authority to interpret truth and communicate it to believers, who accept it on faith.[49]

To de Lamennais that meant the pope, as the head of the Catholic Church, is vested with infallibility in matters of faith, morals, reason, and their application in the social sciences. As far as de Lamennais was concerned, the Will of God as interpreted by the pope is the source of all truth. This contradicts the traditional Catholic position, that God's Nature is reflected in His special creation, man, and discerned by human reason, with which faith is necessarily consistent.[50]

Gardner, "Joachim of Flora," *The Catholic Encyclopedia*, Vol. 8, New York: Robert Appleton and Co., 1913.

[47] Rommen, *The Natural Law, op. cit.*, 51-52; George Weigel, *The Cube and the Cathedral: Europe, America, and Politics Without God.* New York: Basic Books, 2005, 82-86.

[48] Philip Spencer, *Politics of Belief in Nineteenth Century France.* London: Faber and Faber Limited, 1954, 39-40.

[49] Saint John Henry Newman, unaware that the Fathers of the First Vatican Council had explicitly repudiated an exaggerated interpretation of papal infallibility, presented his *Essay in Aid of a Grammar of Assent* (1870) as a clarification of the definition. The *Grammar* had its origin in Newman's efforts during the late 1850s and early 1860s to argue a middle way between those like de Lamennais, who based everything on faith even when it contradicted reason, and those such as his friend William Froude (1810-1879), who rejected faith and believed that theological conclusions reached by human reason were uncertain. Wilfred Ward, *Life of John Henry Cardinal Newman.* London: Longmans, Green, and Co., 1913, II.307; Alejandro Sada Mier y Terán, "The Legitimacy of Certitude in Newman's *Grammar of Assent,*" *Yearbook of the Irish Philosophical Society, 2014/15*, Angelo Bottone, editor. Maynooth, Éire: Irish Philosophical Society, 2015, 49-63.

[50] In Thomist philosophy God is a perfect Being and therefore His Nature is self-realized in His Intellect, that is, all that God is, is consistent with God's reason without any possible contradiction. As they are in perfect union, the action of God's Intellect

In de Lamennais's thought, truth cannot be known by the operation of individual reason on the evidence of the senses guided by faith. Truth is known only by accepting on faith the authority of humanity as a whole as interpreted by the pope.[51] As with the Averroist ideas of Siger of Brabant (*cir.* 1235- *cir.* 1285) in the thirteenth century and those of William of Ockham in the fourteenth century, de Lamennais's theory of certitude meant that the truths of faith and the truths of reason could contradict one another.[52]

Contradicting de Lamennais's own principle of individual sovereignty, the theory of certitude was a restatement of Plato's error that ideas exist independently of the human mind.[53] It led inevitably to the socialist idea that either God grants rights to the collective or the collective self-generates rights, and those in control of the collective then grant rights to actual human beings as expedient or necessary.

The popes were at first inclined to favor de Lamennais for his defense of the rights of the Church against both reactionaries and radicals, and they approved his writings. On reflection, however, the lack of consistency between the ideas of de Lamennais and the newly revived philosophy of Saint Thomas Aquinas (1225-1274) resulted in Pope Gregory XVI (Bartolomeo Alberto Cappellari, 1765-1846, elected 1831) condemning de Lamennais's theories in 1832. This was in *Mirari Vos*, "On Liberalism and Religious Indifferentism," the first social encyclical.

De Lamennais at first submitted, but then he evidently forgot that his own theory gave the pope infallibility in faith, morals, reason, and the application thereof. He became enraged at what he considered the pope's duplicity. This was exacerbated by Gregory's condemnation of the Polish November Uprising of 1830/31.[54]

---

and Will are combined in a single, unified act; for God, to think is to act. God's Will is therefore fully consistent with His Nature. In Catholic belief, human nature is a reflection of God's Nature, thus, anything that purports to be God's Will cannot contradict human nature.

[51] Thomas Bokenkotter, *Church and Revolution: Catholics in the Struggle for Democracy and Social Justice*. New York: Doubleday, 1998, 43-44.

[52] Cf. Adler, *Truth in Religion, op. cit.*, 23-27.

[53] God is absolute truth and therefore exists independently of the human mind, but human ideas and understanding of truth do not exist independently of the minds that create them.

[54] This is another example of a pope's lack of expertise as pope in matters other than faith and morals. The condemnation was politically and religiously necessary due to a forged encyclical in the pope's name calling on people to rebel against Church and State, but this was not mentioned in the condemnation. This gave the pope's action the appearance of being completely arbitrary and opposed to needed reforms.

Repudiating his priesthood and renouncing Christianity, de Lamennais established his own "Religion of Humanity."[55] In 1834 he published a vitriolic pamphlet, *Les Paroles d'un Croyant* ("Words of a Believer") attacking the Church, the pope, kings, and anyone else who did not accept his collectivist version of liberal democracy.

Gregory XVI then issued the second social encyclical, *Singulari Nos* ("On the Errors of Lamennais"), in which he characterized de Lamennais's booklet as "small in size, but great in evil." In the encyclical, the pope also referred to what would become known as socialism, modernism, and New Age thought as *rerum novarum*, "new things."

Within the Thomist framework, what the Catholic Church calls modernism is essentially fideism, as Fulton John Sheen (1895-1979) explained in *God and Intelligence* (1925) and *Religion Without God* (1927). It starts as a shift from reason to faith as the basis of natural law, focuses on collective man instead of God, and generally concludes with the New Age before sliding into some form of spiritualism or secularism and rejecting religious faith altogether.

Broadly speaking, as far as the Catholic Church is concerned, socialism is applied modernism, with the collective created by man taking precedence over man created by God. As Chesterton noted,

> [A]pparently anything can be called Socialism, . . . If it means anything, it seems to mean Modernism; in the sociological as distinct from the theological sense. In both senses, it is generally a euphemism for muddle-headedness.[56]

---

[55] As Alexis de Tocqueville later remarked, de Lamennais had "a pride great enough to walk over the heads of kings and bid defiance to God." Alexis de Tocqueville, *The Recollections of Alexis de Tocqueville*. Cleveland, Ohio: The World Publishing Company, 1959, 191.

[56] G.K. Chesterton, "There Was a Socialist," *G.K.'s Weekly*, May 10, 1930; cf. *Ubi Arcano*, § 61.

2
Something Missing

Despite the best efforts of Pope Pius IX (Giovanni Maria Mastai-Ferretti, 1792-1878, elected 1846), socialism and the other new things continued to spread. Finally, in 1868 he convened the first ecumenical council since Trent in the sixteenth century.

Although the outbreak of the Franco-Prussian War in 1870 abruptly terminated the Council, the Fathers of Vatican I did define two key doctrines that countered de Lamennais's theory of certitude. These were the infallibility of the teaching office of the pope, and the primacy of the intellect.

Infallibility is often misunderstood, even by Catholics. It applies only to matters of faith and morals, and then only under certain conditions. Significantly, infallibility does not apply to any kind of science, including theology, which in the Catholic Church is regarded as the "Queen of the Sciences."[1]

In Catholic belief, a pope guided by the Holy Spirit can be absolutely correct in defining a principle in matters of faith and morals. At the same time, lacking the omniscience of God, he can be completely wrong when applying that same principle to a specific instance or situation. Thus, as was the case with the initial approval of de Lamennais's theory of certitude, a pope can be mistaken when applying his reason to a political, social, scientific, theological, or philosophical question.[2]

One of the purposes in defining papal infallibility was to rein in the extravagant claims of those who, like de Lamennais, imputed far greater power to the pope than that with which, in Catholic belief, his

---

[1] The Medieval appellation. In the early nineteenth century the mathematician Carl Friedrich Gauss called mathematics Queen of the Sciences.

[2] Another example cited to call infallibility into question is Pope Honorius I's hasty approval of the Monothelitist heresy in A.D. 634. That, however, was an imprudent declaration in a theological matter, and did not concern faith or morals directly. Patriarch Sergius of Constantinople proposed Monothelitism, the theory that Jesus has two natures but a single will or "energy" in an effort to unify the Nestorians (who held that Jesus is two persons, one human and one divine), the Monophysites (who held that Jesus has one, divine nature), and the Orthodox (who held the Catholic position that Jesus is a single Person with a divine and a human nature). The theory failed to effect a reconciliation, and only succeeded in adding the element of separating the Will and the Intellect to an already confusing situation.

office vests him.[3] Similarly, defining the primacy of the intellect made it clear that, contrary to the theory of certitude, reason — the foundation of faith — resides in every human person, not in any form of the collective or in the pope as pope.[4]

This reaffirmed a fundamental principle of Thomist philosophy and of Catholic doctrine. That is, knowledge of God's existence and of the natural law written in the hearts of all men can be known by the force and light of human reason alone.[5] As the Council Fathers declared,

> If anyone says that the one, true God, our creator and lord, cannot be known with certainty from the things that have been made,[6] by the natural light of human reason[7]: let him be anathema.[8]

Rerum Novarum

After the death of Pius IX in 1878 the new things of socialism, modernism, and the New Age remained a threat. Nevertheless, Pope Leo XIII (Vincenzo Gioacchino Raffaele Luigi Pecci, 1810-1903, elected 1878) proved a serious disappointment to reactionaries and radicals alike by steering the Church by a middle course into the modern age. Initially, however, even though he issued a series of encyclicals on the problem in the early years of his pontificate, he was not able to make significant headway in countering the new things.

Something was missing from the program. Simply condemning the new things was not having the desired effect. As more and more people were stripped of power, respect for human dignity and the sovereignty of the person continued to degenerate as the nineteenth century wore on.

Fortunately, however, Leo XIII was not only an outstanding philosopher and theologian, he was also a capable civil politician and statesmen. He is the last pope to have had experience of civil government, having served as Papal Governor of Benevento and of Perugia, as well as in the diplomatic corps of the Papal States.

In the 1880s, controversies stirred up in the United States by Father Edward McGlynn (1837-1900) and the adherence of many

---

[3] Ward, *Life of John Henry Cardinal Newman, op. cit.*, II.307.
[4] Cf. *Divini Redemptoris*, § 29: "Only man, the human person, and not society in any form is endowed with reason and a morally free will."
[5] Cf. The Oath Against Modernism and *Humani Generis*, § 2. N.B., this does not mean the Church claims any specific proof of God's existence has been developed — even that of Aquinas — only that it is possible.
[6] That is, by empirical evidence.
[7] That is, by the human intellect.
[8] Vatican I, Canon 2.1.

Catholics to the theories of the agrarian socialist Henry George (1839-1897) threw the Catholic world into confusion. As the situation developed, Leo XIII realized that what was needed was a proactive social program in addition to sound social doctrine to counter the allure of socialism and restore personal economic power as the basis for maintaining essential human dignity. This he presented in 1891 in *Rerum Novarum*, "On Labor and Capital." The pope's prescription can be summed up very briefly:

> We have seen that this great labor question cannot be solved save by assuming as a principle that private ownership must be held sacred and inviolable. The law, therefore, should favor ownership, and its policy should be to induce as many as possible of the people to become owners.[9]

Unfortunately, demonstrating that even someone like Leo XIII can make a mistake in applying a principle, the only suggestion he had as to the means to implement his program was one that virtually guaranteed lack of success. As he said,

> If a workman's wages be sufficient to enable him comfortably to support himself, his wife, and his children, he will find it easy, if he be a sensible man, to practice thrift, and he will not fail, by cutting down expenses, to put by some little savings and thus secure a modest source of income.[10]

Consequently, both capitalists and socialists were able to dismiss the main programmatic application in *Rerum Novarum* on the grounds of alleged impossibility. Some even asserted that Leo XIII changed fundamental Catholic teaching due to their confusing the recommended social program with the mandatory social doctrine. Nor were these the only problems.

Although widespread capital ownership is the best and most direct means of personal economic empowerment, even that left unresolved the problem of the increasing complexity of modern life and the growing powerlessness and alienation of the human person from the social order. In addition to an effective means of acquiring and possessing private property in capital, a new social theory, what Alexis-Charles-Henri Clérel de Tocqueville (1805-1859) characterized as "a new science of politics,"[11] was needed to reconnect people to each other and to the common good. This was the problem of social justice.

---

[9] *Rerum Novarum*, § 46.
[10] *Ibid.*
[11] Alexis de Tocqueville, "Author's Introduction," *Democracy in America, Volume I* (1835).

What Happened to Social Justice

Beginning in or about the 1830s, the term "social justice" came into use. Used at first to denote a great many different theories and concepts, some of them contradictory, socialists began using it to mean any program of material social betterment, especially redistribution of existing wealth.

Redistribution (often misnamed "social justice") was divided into voluntary redistribution or philanthropy, and involuntary redistribution (misnamed "distributive justice"). It is important to note that in the socialist framework, the voluntary good of philanthropy was construed as mandatory. Distributive justice as understood by the socialists was no longer derived from the classical concept of Aristotle and Aquinas.

This requires some explanation. In classical philosophy, distributive justice demands that profits and losses be distributed according to the value of the *pro rata* inputs made by participants in a common economic endeavor.[12] Thus, if *A*, *B*, and *C* contribute labor or capital to the value of $10, $15, and $75, respectively, to a project that yields a profit of $1,000, *A* would receive $100, *B* $150, and *C* $750.

When the common endeavor is the *pólis*, that is, an organized community, distributive justice governs rewards and punishments. It demands that honors and awards be granted by an authority in accordance with the relative merit or due of the recipients as determined by the value of their contribution to the community.[13] Thus, a soldier who has exhibited bravery above and beyond the call of duty is given a Medal of Honor, while a just and competent administrator is granted high office with commensurate pay and benefits.

Some authorities assert that distributive justice includes distribution based on need. Strictly speaking, however, this is not true distributive justice. It is an exception permitted in extreme cases under the "principle of double effect" — that something not evil in and of itself but that causes unintended harm may be permitted for the sake of a good that outweighs the harm.

When the need is dire, and all other recourse has been exhausted, duly constituted authority may redistribute wealth to keep people alive and in reasonable health. This is only categorized under

---

[12] *Ethics*, 1131a15-1131b24; Aquinas, *Commentary Ethics*, Book V, Lect. iv-v, 934-946. Cf. *Compendium of the Social Doctrine of the Church*, § 201.
[13] *Ethics*, V. 3, 4; *Summa* IIa IIae, q. 61, a. 2.

distributive justice by default due to the fact it is a distribution made by authority.[14]

As used by the socialists, however, distributive justice took on a fundamentally different meaning. Taking the exception as the rule and dismissing the chief characteristic of true distributive justice, socialists shifted the basis of out-take from proportionality of *input* on the part of the producer or provider (the justice principle), to *need* on the part of the recipient (the charity principle) in all cases, not just exceptional ones.[15] Instead of "from each according to his ability, to each according to his inputs," the distributive principle became "from each according to his ability, to each according to his needs."[16]

This confused justice, the premier natural virtue, with charity ("caritas"), the premier supernatural virtue.[17] True charity cannot be involuntary or coerced, but by relabeling "charity" as "justice" (which can be compelled), some people believe that distribution on the basis of need *can* be coerced. Uncharitable people thus became "unjust" people, even criminals, for not redistributing their wealth to those in need.

Especially in light of the Thomist revival sponsored by Gregory XVI, it was obvious that involuntary redistribution on the basis of need is neither justice nor charity, but at best a barely tolerable expedient in an emergency. Socialism even distorted the great good of philanthropy, the desire to promote the welfare of humanity in

---

[14] *Rerum Novarum*, § 22; *Catechism of the Catholic Church*, § 2236.

[15] Adam Morris, *American Messiahs: False Prophets of a Damned Nation*. New York: W.W. Norton and Company, 2019, 82-83.

[16] Karl Marx, *Critique of the Gotha Program*. Peking, China: Foreign Languages Press, 1972, 17.

[17] A natural or "cardinal" virtue is one for which every human being has by nature the capacity to acquire and develop. A supernatural or "theological" virtue is one for which God has granted ("infused into") every human being the capacity to acquire and develop. The differences in the natures of the cardinal and the theological virtues in Thomist philosophy is that the latter are not fully accessible to humans in their natural state without assistance from God: "All virtues have as their final scope to dispose man to acts conducive to his true happiness. The happiness, however, of which man is capable is twofold, namely, natural, which is attainable by man's natural powers, and supernatural, which exceeds the capacity of unaided human nature. Since, therefore, merely natural principles of human action are inadequate to a supernatural end, it is necessary that man be endowed with supernatural powers to enable him to attain his final destiny. Now these supernatural principles are nothing else than the theological virtues." (Waldron, Martin Augustine (1912). "Virtue," *The Catholic Encyclopedia*, 15. New York: Robert Appleton Company.) By building the natural virtues, people draw closer to their fellow man. By building the supernatural virtues, people draw closer to God.

general. Socialists confused redistributing wealth for the general welfare with almsgiving, a type of charity to benefit particular individuals.[18]

Countering Socialism

The Catholic response was not long in coming. Having observed the
damage done by mistakes in philosophy, politics, and theology, Monsignor Luigi Aloysius Taparelli d'Azeglio, S.J. (1793-1862) developed
a principle of social justice to correct the errors of the socialists. In
1840 he published *Saggio Teoretico di Dritto Naturale* — "The Theoretical Essay of Natural Law" — to explain his principle.

Socialist "social justice" can be summarized as "the end justifies the
means." Even the principles of natural law, the capacity for which
defines human beings as human beings, can be set aside to achieve
the goal of a better society.

In contrast, in Taparelli's principle of social justice, the end does
not justify the means. Everything, even (or especially) social improvement and the general welfare, must be subordinate to the natural law
as understood in Aristotelian-Thomism, *i.e.*, in Catholic belief, to
God.[19]

This, however, was not a true social ethics, but individual ethics
with a good intention toward the common good.[20] What Taparelli developed was a new principle of social justice as an application of traditional virtues meant to benefit individuals directly, but with a general intention to benefit the whole of society indirectly.

As Aristotle explained in the *Nichomachean Ethics* and the *Politics*,
this is sound guidance for the *bios politikos*, the life of the individual
citizen in the State. It does not, however, address specifically social
problems, such as flaws in our institutions that inhibit or prevent the
exercise of individual virtue.

Most (if not all) of the confusion over social justice results from generations of scholars and advocates attempting to resolve the socialist
and the Taparelli versions of social justice and synthesize a consistent definition. Obviously, however, a theory of social justice that
says the natural law is subordinate to the will of the people

---

[18] There is, of course, a great deal of overlap between philanthropy and charity, with
specific instances often difficult to categorize. For analytical purposes, however, philanthropy is construed as a general virtue, while charity is construed as a particular
virtue.

[19] Rommen, *The Natural Law, op. cit.*, 45.

[20] Ferree, *Introduction to Social Justice, op. cit.*, 10.

(socialism), and one that says the will of the people is subordinate to the natural law (Taparelli) can never be reconciled. Any attempt to do so, or even define it in any meaningful way, can only result in contradiction.

Essentially, Taparelli's work did no more than restate traditional moral philosophy. As such, it was no more effective at countering socialism and the other new things than papal condemnations had been. Social justice remained, by and large, a euphemism for socialism,[21] and people continued to be alienated from society at an accelerating rate.

The Act of Social Justice

In such an environment, new forms of socialism appeared with increasing frequency, each attempting to correct the flaws of all the others, each claiming to be different, and yet all indistinguishable in substance. As de Tocqueville noted of the 1848 French Revolution,

> From the 25th of February [1848] onwards, a thousand strange systems came issuing pell-mell from the minds of innovators, and spread among the troubled minds of the crowd. . . . These theories were of very varied natures, often opposed and sometimes hostile to one another; but all of them, aiming lower than the government and striving to reach society itself, on which government rests, adopted the common name of Socialism.[22]

There were thus two elements lacking in Catholic social teaching essential to reconnecting people as sovereign persons to each other in society. These were, one, a means of direct access by each person to the common good and all institutions of the social order. Two, a viable means of empowering each human person economically through direct ownership of productive assets ("capital") to make that full social access effective.

In *Rerum Novarum*, Leo XIII seems to have assumed that both issues could easily be resolved. He appeared to take for granted that the common good can be accessed by organizing and having a general intention to benefit the common good. He also supposed that

---

[21] There are only two known Curial uses of the term social justice prior to the pontificate of Pius XI, and they were consistent with Taparelli's notion of social justice as a principle applying individual virtues rather than a particular virtue directed to the common good. These were in 1894 in a reference to the demand for reparation when another is harmed (*Acta Sanctae Sedis*, 1894-1895, 131) and by St. Pius X in a 1904 encyclical when he stated St. Gregory the Great was a defender of social justice (*Iucunda Sane*, § 3).

[22] De Tocqueville, *Recollections, op. cit.*, 78-79.

widespread capital ownership could be financed by paying workers more, thus allowing them to save to buy capital. Both assumptions were incorrect.

As a result, most authorities and many people failed to grasp the significance of Leo's social doctrine and its application in a social program. Capitalists reinterpreted Leo's encyclical as a capitalist tract, while socialists considered it a new manifesto for their cause.[23]

With the pontificate of Pius XI (Ambrogio Damiano Achille Ratti, 1857-1939; elected 1922) one of the missing pieces in Leo XIII's thought was addressed. This was through Pius XI's development of a doctrine of social virtue explaining how the human person gains direct access to the common good.

In Pius XI's thought, traditional individual virtues benefit individuals directly, and society indirectly. Social virtues, on the other hand, benefit society directly, but individuals indirectly.

Through acts of social virtue, human persons can effect necessary changes directly in the social environment — "the system" — conforming the institutions of the common good more closely to human nature. This establishes and maintains the proper environment for becoming virtuous. People can more easily become more fully human, because the system encourages them to become virtuous.

For many years prior to his election Pius XI had made an in-depth study of Taparelli's work. Developing Taparelli's principle, the pope appears to have realized that it is possible to bring the human person together with others in solidarity. Significantly, *solidarity* is not a mere feeling, but acceptance and internalization of the principles that define a group as that specific group.

Through organized action directed at building or perfecting the common good, people can secure their natural rights and restructure institutions to conform to human nature as far as possible. The work of social justice never ends, because institutions as human creations can never be perfect.

This is in sharp contrast to the principles of socialism that seek to absorb or subsume the human person into the State or collective. Socialism tries to change human nature by abolishing natural rights and conforming it to "ideal" institutions as defined by some *élite*.[24]

---

[23] See, *e.g.*, Vicomte Eugène Melchior de Vogüé, "The Neo-Christian Movement in France," *Harper's New Monthly Magazine*, Vol. 84, No. 500, January 1892, 234-242.
[24] Significantly, Pope Leo XII (Annibale Francesco Clemente Melchiorre Girolamo Nicola Sermattei della Genga, 1760-1829, elected 1823) said of de Lamennais, "He is an

Leo XIII's program in *Rerum Novarum* took for granted what individualists and collectivists alike did not even consider possible: that people can directly access and reform the common good. Pius XI's breakthrough in moral philosophy was *the recognition of social justice as a particular virtue directed to the common good with a defined act of its own.* This resolved one of the major difficulties with the social program (as distinct from the social doctrine) of Leo XIII.

Building on Leo XIII's thought in this manner was a major advance in developing a sound theory of personalism consistent with natural law and Aristotelian-Thomist philosophy. *Personalism* being any school of thought or intellectual movement that *focuses on the reality of the human person and each person's unique dignity,*[25] it demands that *the institutions of the common good be equally accessible by every natural person,* i.e., by every human being, and thus that every person have power.

Full and direct access to the common good in turn requires more than every person being able to exercise the full spectrum of the classic individual virtues[26] and rights.[27] This is because individual virtues and rights only grant indirect access to the common good. A holistic understanding of rights and virtues at both the individual and social levels, however, requires that each person have direct access to the common good and all its institutions through the free exercise of the *social virtues,* especially social charity and social justice.

Two factors seem to have kept people from understanding the social virtues as something distinct from the individual virtues. First and foremost is the failure to realize that the social virtues are not directed to individual goods or natural persons.

Social virtues (acts or habits) are directed to the "objects" of the common good and "artificial persons"[28] — institutions that affect

---

esaltato, a distinguished man of talents, knowledge, and good faith. But he is one of those lovers of perfection who, if one should leave them alone, would overthrow the whole world." Dudon, *Lamennais et le Saint-Siège* (Paris, 1911), 29; quoted in Heinrich Rommen, *The State in Catholic Thought: A Treatise in Political Philosophy.* St. Louis, Missouri: B. Herder Book Co., 1947, 436n.

[25] Williams, "What is Thomistic Personalism?" *loc. cit.*

[26] Specified in Thomism as the natural virtues of prudence, temperance, fortitude, and justice, and the supernatural virtues of faith, hope, and charity.

[27] The natural rights of life, liberty, and private property.

[28] Applying the term "person" to things is problematical, especially when the subject is personalism, which in the context of this discussion regards only the human person as a person, strictly speaking. There is also the issue that in terms of the social virtues *all* organizations are "artificial persons," or they could not be the directed objects of virtues. This is complicated by the fact that in law, an "artificial person" is a legal

persons. Second, the efficient cause or *subject* (that which carries out the act of a virtue) of both individual virtue and social virtue is the human person.

There is, however, a difference between the efficient cause of an individual virtue and that of a social virtue. Where the efficient cause (that which carries out the act) of an individual virtue is the individual person as an individual, the efficient cause of a social virtue is the individual person *as a member of a group*. As Father William Ferree explained,

> It is surely nothing new to suggest that man is the efficient cause of the act of social justice; but something that has not been sufficiently adverted to is that *only the member of a group* is capable of such an act. A completely isolated individual *cannot* practice social justice, even though he be a man in possession of all his powers. . . . *All men*, utterly regardless of any theories Aristotle may have had about foreigners, resident aliens, slaves, mechanics, and laborers, are efficient causes of social justice, insofar as they can perform any act of virtue, *i.e.*, be in possession of the "use of reason" and exercise of their will.[29]

Pius XI's social doctrine thereby solved one of the most serious problems of modern life: the powerlessness and thus alienation of the human person from society — but with one critical omission. Social justice and its commanded act told precisely the theoretical *who*, *what*, *when*, *where*, and *why*, but it left the practical *how* incomplete.

The Question of Money

Pius XI, Leo XIII, and generations of political philosophers and moralists agreed in general how people are to become more fully human and also reform society. Historically, most authorities have concurred that widespread capital ownership is essential if people are to have the personal power they need to carry out acts of virtue and so become more fully human. Social justice adds the necessity of personal power to be able to organize in free association with others to effect necessary changes in institutions and the common good as a whole.

Unfortunately, not being experts in money, credit, banking, and finance, the best the popes could do was to recommend that workers be paid more. This would presumably enable them to save and finally

---

fiction that applies only to certain forms of organization. This adds confusion to an already complex analysis, but it is the accepted terminology at present and will be used in lieu of anything better.
[29] Rev. William J. Ferree, S.M., Ph.D., *The Act of Social Justice*. Washington, DC: The Catholic University of America Press, 1942 (© 1943), 194-195.

purchase capital to supplement and in some cases replace wage income, and gain control over their own lives.[30]

It is true that it is possible for workers to exercise the required thrift and accumulate enough savings to purchase capital. It is, however, not probable on the individual level, nor realistic for an entire economy.

At the individual level, raising wages without a commensurate expansion of production increases the cost of production, and thus raises prices to the consumer. Since the consumer is in most cases the wage earner himself and his dependents, any wage increase is usually cancelled out by the increase in prices.[31]

At the level of an entire economy, financing capital formation (i.e., acquiring capital) by reducing consumption and accumulating savings creates an "economic dilemma." As explained by Dr. Harold Glenn Moulton (1883-1965), president of the Brookings Institution in Washington, DC from 1928 to 1952, "The dilemma may be summarily stated as follows: In order to accumulate money savings, we must decrease our expenditures for consumption; but in order to expand capital goods *profitably*, we must increase our expenditures for consumption."[32]

That is (as Moulton went on), if people reduce their consumption to save to finance capital acquisition, there will not be enough consumer demand to justify investing in new capital. Thus, as Moulton noted,

> If a larger percentage of the national income is saved, we have abundance of funds with which to create new capital; but such capital is not profitable. If, on the other hand, a larger percentage is diverted to consumption channels it is profitable to construct new plant and equipment; but there are inadequate funds for the purpose.[33]

Fortunately, Moulton then went on to explain how relying on savings generated by reducing consumption in the past is not the way that new capital has typically been financed, especially during periods of rapid economic growth. Instead, the bulk of new capital formation at such times has been financed by expanding commercial bank credit backed by increasing production in the future.

---

[30] *Rerum Novarum*, § 46; *Quadragesimo Anno*, §§ 61, 63.
[31] It is actually worse in most cases. Factors in addition to wage increases cause a rise in the price level, especially when governments back the currency with their own debt to monetize deficits. Real income declines.
[32] Harold G. Moulton, *The Formation of Capital*. Washington, DC: The Brookings Institution, 1935, 28.
[33] *Ibid.*, 35.

Commercial banking and the entire science of finance, in fact, are based on knowing the distinction between the different types of savings and their proper uses to back the different types of money.[34] "Past savings" generated by reducing consumption is best used for consumption. "Future savings" generated by increasing production is best used for financing new capital to increase production. Finally, backing the money supply with government debt — "no savings" — is best used for nothing at all.

Moulton thereby demonstrated that new capital can be financed without reducing consumption or increasing wages when there is no commensurate increase in labor productiveness. He did not, however, make what in Catholic social teaching or the Just Third Way seems the obvious correlation, that here also was a just and feasible means to finance widespread capital ownership without redistribution.[35]

It was not until Louis Orth Kelso (1913-1991) and Mortimer Adler published *The Capitalist Manifesto* (1958)[36] and *The New Capitalists* (1961)[37] that a viable and personalist means of bringing about widespread capital ownership became known to the general public. The subtitle of the second volume is significant: "A Proposal to Free Economic Growth from the Slavery of Savings."

Kelso — Adler gave him full credit for the idea[38] — did not mean that capital can be formed without the use of savings. As noted above, Moulton pointed out that savings can be generated either by reducing consumption (past savings) or by increasing production (future savings). What Kelso meant was, instead of people working to accumulate savings, future savings (meaning future profits used to pay off a capital loan) could work for people to accumulate capital.

Considered as a breakthrough in applying moral philosophy (which is what primarily interested Adler) Kelso's achievement was to

---

[34] Put another way, "The first principle of commercial banking is to know 'the difference between a bill of exchange and a mortgage'." Benjamin M. Anderson, *Economics and the Public Welfare: A Financial and Economic History of the United States, 1914-1946.* Indianapolis, Indiana: Liberty Fund, Inc., 1980, 233.

[35] Moulton (or, perhaps more fairly, his associates at the Brookings Institution) assumed as a matter of course that widespread capital ownership means redistribution of existing capital assets, not participation in the financing and thus ownership of new capital assets. Harold G. Moulton, *Income and Economic Progress.* Washington, DC: The Brookings Institution, 1935, 76.

[36] Louis O. Kelso and Mortimer J. Adler, *The Capitalist Manifesto.* New York: Random House, 1958.

[37] Louis O. Kelso and Mortimer J. Adler, *The New Capitalists: A Proposal to Free Economic Growth from the Slavery of Savings.* New York: Random House, 1961.

[38] Kelso and Adler, *The Capitalist Manifesto, op. cit.,* ix.

explain how techniques of modern corporate finance could be used to provide money and credit to make every person an owner of capital without redistribution or harming private property in any way. Expansion of commercial bank credit backed up by a central bank and collateralized with capital credit insurance could be used to provide full access to capital ownership by every member of society.

Nor was that all. Kelso's breakthrough was not merely to develop a new application of the science of finance. His innovative financing techniques were, instead, a logical development of the principles of economic justice presented in Chapter 5 of *The Capitalist Manifesto*.[39] Kelso along with Adler[40] developed three principles of economic justice:

- **The Principle of Participation.** "[E]veryone has a right to earn a living by participating in the production of wealth,"[41] whether through one's contribution of labor or one's capital.

- **The Principle of Distribution.** "[E]ach should receive a share that is proportionate to the value of the contribution each has made to the production of that wealth."[42]

- **The Principle of Limitation.** "[T]he ownership of productive property by an individual or household must not be allowed to increase beyond the point where it injures others by excluding them from the opportunity to earn a viable income."[43]

This was the final piece of the puzzle that had baffled so many people, and that, in an effort to circumvent natural law and even revelation, had resulted in the development and growth of socialism, modernism, and New Age thought. With Kelso's breakthrough combined with that of Pius XI, Catholic social teaching had the potential to become an effective personalism in practice as well as in theory, an applied economic personalism consistent with a sound Thomist philosophy of personalism.

---

[39] *Ibid.*, 52-86.
[40] As noted, Adler credited Kelso with the ideas, but Adler was probably responsible for the rigorous analysis and systematic presentation of the ideas of economic justice in *The Capitalist Manifesto*.
[41] *Ibid.* 68. CESJ has refined and developed the principle of participation into "participative justice," recognizing it as a particular virtue.
[42] *Ibid.*, 67. CESJ recognizes the principle of distribution as classical "distributive justice." Distributive justice guides not only transactions among individuals, but also the structuring and operation of institutions.
[43] *Ibid.* CESJ has expanded Kelso and Adler's principle of limitation to the much broader particular virtue of social justice. This relates not only to the balance and harmony of participative and distributive justice, but also to the act of organizing to correct unjust or defective institutions.

3
A Theory of Human Dignity

Human dignity is the focus of Catholic social teaching, as it is for every other personalist system, program, faith, or philosophy. In Catholic teaching as well as in many other faiths and philosophies, the human person is a special creation of God, differing both in degree and in kind from every other creature, whether sentient, animate, or inanimate.[1]

Especially as developed by Karol Wojtyła specifically within the framework of Aristotelian-Thomism and Catholic social teaching, personalism focuses on the reality of the human person and each person's unique dignity.[2] Our fellow man therefore has a special claim on our consideration. As Mortimer Adler explained in a lecture on human nature he delivered at the Aspen Institute in 1989,

> [L]et me repeat once more the difference between human nature and that of all other animal species. In the case of other animal species, the specific nature common to all members of the species is constituted mainly by quite determinate[3] characteristics or attributes. In the case of the human species, it is constituted by determinable characteristics or attributes. An innate potentiality is precisely that: something determinable, not wholly determinate, and determinable in a wide variety of ways.[4]

Adler's "innate potentiality" is the capacity that each human being has by nature to become virtuous, the habit of doing good, with good discernible by the use of human reason. Ultimately, this is the good common to every human being that unites every member of the human race, and it was the starting point for Wojtyła's analysis.

Further, Adler noted that man's intellect and free will are what give him the potential that makes him different from all other temporal beings. Every person also has inalienable rights to realize that potential.[5] He concluded,

---

[1] *Ut Unum Sint*, § 28.
[2] Thomas D. Williams, L.C., "What is Thomistic Personalism?" *Alpha Omega*, Vol. VII, No. 2, 2004, 164.
[3] The text reads "determinable," capable of being determined or decided upon. This makes no sense in the context of the lecture and the succeeding sentences, so it has been changed to "determinate," having defined limits.
[4] Adler, *Truth in Religion, op. cit.*, 154.
[5] *Ibid.*, 151-152.

All the cultural and nurtural differences that separate one human sub-
group from another are superficial as compared with the underlying
common human nature that unites the members of mankind. . . . There
is only a human mind and it is one and the same in all human beings.[6]

The Theory of Personalism

One of the first points we realize about personalism is that it is not,
strictly speaking, a philosophy in the usual academic meaning of the
term, *i.e.*, a system of philosophical concepts, such as Thomism or
Platonism. That is why Wojtyła framed his thought within the context of the philosophy of Aquinas.

In the thought of Wojtyła, personalism is a way of thinking based
on a specific set of principles and assumptions. It enables us to approach or evaluate a philosophy to see how well — or if — it conforms
to what are in Catholic belief the particular, even unique needs of
every human being as a human person and special creation of God.
Wojtyła's personalism brings together the concrete, objective reality
of each human person, and the abstract, theoretical-moral plane of
metaphysics (that is, the natural law) to reconcile the actual to the
ideal and bring them together to mutual advantage.[7]

If an interpretation of a doctrine or principle of a faith or philosophy
that claims to be personalist results in a failure to respect the dignity
of every human person, that interpretation is by definition incorrect
or faulty. As Wojtyła and others have realized, personalism and human dignity are inseparable concepts; one is incomplete without the
other.

Begging the question, we defined personalism in Chapter 1, but
only in terms of human dignity. We need now to look at what we mean
by human dignity, while avoiding an understanding that is either collectivist or individualist.

In common with Wojtyła, we begin with the question, What is "dignity"? As defined in the dictionary, dignity is the "quality or state of
being worthy, honored, or esteemed."[8] From the standpoint of inalienable rights, dignity is the right of a person to be valued and respected for his own sake, and to be treated with justice.[9] In Thomist
philosophy, every single human being, because he is a human being,

---

[6] *Ibid.*, 155-156.
[7] Svidercoschi, *Stories of Karol, op. cit.* 139-140.
[8] "Dignity," *Meriam-Webster Dictionary*.
[9] Cf. "Person," *Black's Law Dictionary*.

is automatically a person, and therefore "worthy, honored, or esteemed."

This definition of dignity is fully consistent with the Thomist concept of personalism as used in the Just Third Way. We must specify the Thomist concept of personalism because there are other, competing versions of personalism, such as those of Emmanuel Mounier (1905-1950) and Max Ferdinand Scheler (1874-1928), that differ materially from the principles of Aristotelian-Thomism, and thus from the thought of Wojtyła.

Respect for human dignity is not based on wealth, poverty, race, religion, sexual orientation, or other accidental characteristics.[10] Rather, in Catholic belief respect for human dignity is realized through recognition and protection of the sovereignty of each human person under the ultimate sovereignty of God, and that means recognition and protection of each person's fundamental rights and place in society.

Since personalism encompasses numerous, sometimes even divergent schools of thought,[11] it is sometimes difficult to decide what constitutes a standard personalist way of thinking. Limiting ourselves to a Thomist framework, as did Wojtyła, the task becomes easier, as there are characteristics of personalism as defined by Thomist personalists with which others usually agree:

- **Binary Character.** All persons are distinct from things.
- **Human Dignity.** All persons have rights by nature and are individually sovereign under the highest sovereignty of God.
- **Determinable Instead of Determinate Nature.** All persons have determinable characteristics; all things have determinate characteristics.
- **Self-Determination.** All persons have free will.
- **Political Animals.** All persons associate by nature within a consciously structured social order.

Binary Character. As analyzed within a Catholic framework, personalism presupposes the existence of God, and thus assigns a unique character to human beings, God's special creation. Personalist

---

[10] Rufus Burrow, Jr., *God and Human Dignity*. Notre Dame, Indiana: University of Notre Dame Press, 2006, 165.
[11] In 1946 Jacques Maritain wrote that "[t]here are, at least, a dozen personalist doctrines, which, at times, have nothing more in common than the word 'person'." Jacques Maritain, *The Person and the Common Good*. Notre Dame, Indiana: University of Notre Dame Press, 1966, 13.

thought therefore sees two types of relationships in society — relationships to other persons, and relationships to things.[12] (We will not, of course, discuss the religious aspects of personalism, as those are faith-based.)

Human beings as persons are both subjects and objects; we are both that which acts (subject), and that which is acted upon (object). Human beings are therefore somebodies instead of somethings, and we relate to one another by the interplay of rights and duties. A right is the power to do or not do some act or acts in relation to other persons, while a duty is the obligation to do or not do some act or acts in relation to other persons.

Relations to things are not the same as they are to persons. Not being subjects, things have no rights, but persons as subjects have rights to and over things that define their relationships to other persons with respect to things.[13]

Things, even artificial persons such as corporations and governments, are only objects, that which is related by intention to a subject. Objects can only act (in the philosophical sense) through human agents, and not of their own volition.

Human Dignity. Because the human person is unique in creation, Thomist personalism divides reality into persons (which have dignity) and non-persons (which do not have dignity). Relations with persons therefore require a different ethical paradigm, an entirely different set of rules, than that which governs mere objects. Principally, this means that persons are entitled to justice, a rendering to each what each is due.

Traditional moral systems put great emphasis on the subject, that is, the moral agent that carries out an act. This is carried to an extreme in Stoicism, in which there is a complete separation of the human person as the object of virtue, from the same person as the subject of virtue. Ideally, the Stoic as object regards everything that happens to him, good or bad, with complete indifference. At the same time, the Stoic as subject is supposed to act virtuously in all relations with others.

---

[12] Cf. Hohfeld, *Fundamental Legal Conceptions, op. cit.*
[13] A thing can be treated as a person, as with the legal fiction called a corporation. Conversely, a person can be treated as a thing called a slave. Aristotle described a slave as an animate tool without the capacity to acquire and develop virtue. *Politics*, 1253b; 1260b, 1-2. For the purposes of this discussion, we take as a given that chattel slavery is incompatible with personalist thought.

As Wojtyła emphasized, however, personalism takes into consideration the transcendent character of human actions and human dignity as they relate to persons as both subject and object. This vests each human being in his capacity as either subject or object with an absolute character as a human person.

Each human being is therefore not only required to act as a person (duty), but he is entitled to be treated as such (right). This implies there are moral absolutes that govern our relations with other persons, even in the so-called social sciences where norms have traditionally been considered arbitrary or merely expedient.

Determinable Instead of Determinate Nature. Where all things conform to their common nature with only minor variations, human nature is such that by free exercise of rights, human beings as persons make choices. As a result of conscious decisions, persons become virtuous or vicious, thus becoming more or less fully human.

Self-Determination. As persons, human beings are responsible for their own acts; we are all in that sense "self-made men." This is because the human person is a rational animal who when educated properly can distinguish truth and falsehood as well as good and evil. Further, because the human person has a spiritual nature, the motivation to act virtuously or viciously is internal instead of being imposed externally, even if we subside within (live in or inhabit) what Wojtyła referred to as "structures of sin."[14]

Political Animals. Human persons are naturally members of society, neither isolated individuals nor indistinguishable members of the collective. We are beings who relate to others in a consciously structured manner as an essential aspect of what and who we are.

Taking into consideration a Catholic framework and these characteristics of Thomist personalist thought, a paradox presents itself. As a person, each human being belongs to himself as an independent and sovereign being under the highest sovereignty of God in a way that a thing cannot.

At the same time, individual sovereignty and man's political nature necessarily imply that each person has the same dignity and status as all other persons. This allows for a giving of one's self to all other persons in society, which could not happen if each person did not possess himself as a sovereign being in the first place.

---

[14] *Evangelium Vitae*, § 24.

Consequently, while all persons have rights absolutely, no one may exercise rights without limits, for that would infringe on the sovereignty of everyone else. As Wojtyła's analysis made clear, there must be a give-and-take in social life, which would not be possible if human beings were isolated individuals or indistinguishable members of the collective.

Economic Personalism and the Just Third Way

Based on the dignity of the human person as a special creation of God, the Just Third Way at the level of economic justice combines the economic justice principles discerned by Louis Kelso and Mortimer Adler in *The Capitalist Manifesto* and the financial techniques described in *The New Capitalists*, with Pius XI's breakthrough in moral philosophy described primarily in *Quadragesimo Anno* and *Divini Redemptoris*[15] and the personalism of Wojtyła. As a free market system economically empowering every human person within a realistic personalist framework, the Just Third Way offers a logical alternative to both individualistic capitalism and collectivistic socialism.

The Just Third Way promotes the formation of structures of virtue in the common good to encourage individual virtue. This is through the systematic diffusion of power and extension of equal capital ownership opportunities to every person, together with the institutional means of acquiring and possessing private property in capital. Encouraging individual virtue by creating systems, structures, and processes that encourage habits of doing good, the Just Third Way conforms to the demands of personalism and respect for human dignity.

Kelso's division of the economic factors of production into the human and the non-human — persons and things — has raised some controversy among traditional economists. Nevertheless, Kelso's emphasis on widespread capital ownership as a fundamental human right and the necessity for a free, non-monopolistic, and just market economy is fully consistent with what Wojtyła emphasized in personalist thought, including the fundamental distinction between that which is a person by nature,[16] and everything else.

Personalism's binary character finds expression in the fact that relations to persons are fundamentally different from relations to things. Kelso's thought recognizes the inherent distinction between

---

[15] See Ferree, *The Act of Social Justice, op. cit., Introduction to Social Justice, op. cit.*
[16] Corporations are "artificial persons," legal fictions created by human beings as social tools. They are not persons by nature.

labor (all human factors of production) and capital (all non-human factors of production).

In what by coincidence Kelso eventually called binary economics, labor is the intrinsic, human factor of production. That is, labor is an inherent part of the human person and cannot be separated from him. Capital is the extrinsic, non-human factor of production. That is, capital is not an inherent part of the human person and can be separated from him. Nevertheless, both labor and capital can be productive, and production means exactly the same thing in both cases, whether the result of labor or of capital.

Further, both labor and capital are owned, and ownership also means exactly the same in both cases. That is, whether labor or capital is used to produce marketable goods and services, the owner has the right to use and dispose of the product of his ownership within the bounds of reason (not harming others or their property) and the demands of the common good.

Our relation as persons to things is called ownership, and consists of private property, that is, the right to be an owner (which includes everybody), and the bundle of rights that define how what is owned can be used (which excludes everybody but the owner). In both personalism and the Just Third Way, persons own their own labor and can own capital, but they cannot own other persons. Persons own, while things are owned.

Thus, while the Just Third Way encompasses far more than economic personalism *per se*, it is fully compatible with respect for the dignity God gave every human person that is the essence of Catholic Thomist personalism. This is best illustrated in the manner the Just Third Way not only enables, but it requires what Wojtyła made the centerpiece of his thought: the gift of self that is at the heart of personalism.[17]

The Gift of Self

As noted above, persons as political animals become most truly themselves by participating in the life of the *pólis* in a manner that benefits both themselves as persons and the common good as a thing, and thus other persons within the common good. Specifically, as Wojtyła implied, in personalist and economic terms (as opposed to mystical and religious) the gift of self is conveyed in two ways, one individual, and one social.

---

[17] *Ut Unum Sint, loc. cit.; Gratissimam Sane,* § 14.

Individually, the gift of self consists of acting virtuously, doing good by and for one's self and particular others directly, but always with an indirect concern for the common good, and thus for others in general. This means at least doing no harm to others or to the common good as a whole, and at most helping to create a culture of virtue by example within the common good.

Socially, the gift of self consists of organizing with others and acting directly on the institutions of the common good to reform them to create structures of virtue. The goal is to provide an environment suitable for the creation of a culture of virtue.

Thus, the gift of self in the Just Third Way consists, one, of acts of individual virtue that benefit the person directly. This allows each person to become more fully himself and benefits the common good indirectly, giving to others by setting a good example.

Two, the gift of self in the Just Third Way also consists of acts of social virtue that benefit the common good directly. Acts of social virtue allow persons as members of organized groups to become more fully members of society, and also to benefit individuals indirectly by providing a suitable environment for the acquisition and development of individual virtue.

Schematic: The Gift of Self		
Subject (Efficient Cause)	Direct Object of Virtue	Indirect Object of Virtue
Individual as Individual	The Human Person	The Common Good
Individual as Member of a Group	The Common Good	The Human Person

Whether carrying out individual or social acts of virtue, the ordinary means of economically empowering persons both as individuals and as members of groups is private property in capital.[18] The recognition of equal access to private property in productive capital as a universal human right is a crucial difference between the Just Third Way and both capitalism and socialism.

In capitalism, ownership of capital is concentrated in a relatively tiny *élite*, limiting the ability of persons to relate to others in society

---

[18] *Laborem Exercens*, § 15.

as persons of equal dignity. In socialism, the collective owns or controls capital, abolishing or controlling the ability of persons to participate in society.

In the Just Third Way, widespread capital ownership links every human being to the common good by securing all other rights and their status as free persons. Thus, economic democracy provides the material foundation of political democracy. By enabling all persons to meet their most basic human needs, widespread capital ownership also provides the opportunity and means for each person to become virtuous, thereby becoming more fully human — the goal of personalism.

Personalism and Catholic Social Teaching

Wojtyła stressed the fact that personalism recognizes a radical distinction between persons and things, the latter category consisting of other beings and non-persons.[19] This is important, because the distinction between persons and things opposes what may be one of the most serious errors of the modern age, and one that has inhibited or prevented many people from understanding Catholic social teaching. That is the failure to distinguish between actual human beings as persons, and collective humanity or "the People," which is an abstraction — a thing.

Demonstrating the universality (catholicity) of a natural law understanding of personalism, that of Dr. Martin Luther King, Jr. supports the Thomist focus on the dignity of the human person. Although he came from a different religious and philosophical tradition, King viewed personalism as a practical means of eradicating injustice, but always consistent with the demands of human dignity and the principles of natural law.[20]

King put special emphasis on eliminating racism and establishing justice through equal opportunity. As he said, "I have the audacity to believe that peoples everywhere can have three meals a day for their bodies, education and culture for their minds, and dignity, equality, and freedom for their spirits."[21]

King's personalism was rooted in his conviction that morality is ultimately the most practical, even expedient alternative, given his acceptance of a transcendent God Who, nevertheless, has a personal

---

[19] *Ibid.*, 179.
[20] Burrow, *God and Human Dignity, op. cit.*, 69.
[21] Acceptance speech for the Nobel Peace Prize, December 10, 1964.

relationship with His special creation, man. Simply imposing desired results regardless of the means was inconsistent with King's moral and political sense as well as contrary to his understanding of the relation of the human person to God and to other people in relation to God.[22]

King's practical personalism therefore involves introducing changes to the social order by reforming institutions through organized non-violent action for the common good. This agrees with Catholic social doctrine that has the goal of reforming institutions to make it possible for people to live virtuously.

Similarly, personalism as Wojtyła conceived it does not contradict or present an alternative to Catholic social teaching, especially that of Pope Leo XIII and Pius XI. Rather, Wojtyła's thought reaffirms the truth of Catholic social teaching. His presumably innovative implementation of the reforms of Vatican II[23] are a textbook example of the techniques and goals of Pius XI's Catholic Action.

Wojtyła's personalism reaffirms Catholic social teaching by making explicit what was implied, and by providing new insights into the profundity of Catholic social thought. This counters superficial and antipersonalist interpretations imposed by adherents of the "new things."

This is especially the case in regard to the correlation of personalism's gift of self with Pius XI's doctrine of social virtue. What Wojtyła called the gift or giving of one's self is not a slogan, poetic metaphor, platitude, or — as he made clear — a way of justifying any form of socialism or collectivism.

Giving of one's self is a key element in Wojtyła's personalism. It is (and can only be) the act of organizing with others to benefit the common good that is the essence of Pius XI's social doctrine.

Using Father Ferree's analysis, we can easily draw the now-obvious correlation between the act of social charity and the gift of self. The act of social charity is loving our institutions as we love ourselves, and our neighbor as ourselves, while recognizing their flaws and seeking their perfection. Giving of one's self to others and to the whole of the common good is manifestly the act of social charity.

How the gift of self makes each of us more fully human is even more obvious once we realize the true character of social justice. The act of social justice (as opposed to acts of individual justice) does not consist

---

[22] Burrow, *God and Human Dignity*, *op. cit.*, 70.
[23] John O'Sullivan, *The President, the Pope, and the Prime Minister: Three Who Changed the World*. Washington, DC: The Regnery Publishing Company, Inc., 2006, 7.

of others providing directly for our individual wants and needs. Neither is it us providing directly for the wants and needs of others. Rather, the act of social justice consists of organizing and working with others to make it possible for everyone to provide for his own wants and needs through his own efforts.

Social justice thereby assists each person in becoming more fully human by becoming more virtuous — but only if we have first given of ourselves to others through acts of social charity and of social justice. In Pius XI's social doctrine this is done by organizing with others for the common good with the goal of removing barriers that inhibit or prevent every person from having full access to the institutions of the common good.

Emphasizing the importance of a Just Third Way perspective on Catholic social teaching, adherents of the new things have in general misunderstood the true nature of social justice. They have failed to correlate Wojtyła's personalism with Pius XI's social doctrine accurately.

Evidently not realizing that personalism amplifies and explains the concept of social justice within the framework provided by a Thomist understanding of the moral absolutes of natural law, socialists, modernists, and New Agers have (probably unconsciously) reinterpreted personalism. By shifting away from the human person created by God, to the abstraction of humanity created by man, they conform to the basic precept of socialism, that all that exists, even the moral absolutes of the natural law on which personalism is grounded, is subordinate to what is desired.

In this way the gift of one's self (charity) changes by degrees into a gift of one's wealth (philanthropy), and the gift of one's wealth into a demand for coercive redistribution of the wealth of others (socialism). To correct what should be an obvious error, we have to go beyond merely defining personalism as we have done in this chapter. We need to understand the elements of that definition — its concepts of good (both individual and common), private property, what it means to be a political animal, even what happiness is and what it means to become more fully human and thus a better or more complete person.

4
Seeking the Good

In the American Declaration of Independence, Thomas Jefferson (1743-1826) stated that all people are endowed by their Creator with certain inalienable rights, among which are life, liberty, and the pursuit of happiness. This statement is key to understanding the Declaration and thus the philosophy of personalism that provided the basis for American liberal democracy.

Only persons have rights, and since human beings have rights by nature, we are therefore natural persons.

A startling omission from Jefferson's list is private property. Slavery (human beings owned as chattels, *i.e.*, non-land possessions) was a serious bone of contention among the members of the Continental Congress.

Jefferson himself took a position that could charitably be described as hypocritical, condemning slavery, declaring he was resolved to free his slaves, but then not doing so. Given the Founders' inability to reconcile the irreconcilable, omitting private property from the list of natural rights in the Declaration of Independence was understandable — not forgivable, but understandable.

What is Good?

What, however, did Jefferson mean by "pursuit of happiness"? To begin, we cannot understand happiness without understanding what is good.

According to Aristotle, all that exists seeks the good. If someone seeks that which is not good or is evil, it is because he either has a distorted idea of good, or he is trying to avoid a greater evil.

This leads to the question, what is good, and what does it mean to seek the good?

If we assume that an all-good and perfect Creator made all that exists, then good consists of what the Creator made. We would otherwise have to assume the impossible and say that an all-good and perfect Creator could contradict His own Nature (*i.e.*, be an imperfect perfect Being) and create that which is not good or is even evil.

This gives us a definition of good: that which is in conformity with nature. What is good for a dog is to conform to the nature of a dog.

What is good for a cat is to conform to the nature of a cat. What is good for a human being is to conform to human nature.

This creates a problem, at least for human beings. While it seems that all we see around us conforms to its own nature as a matter of course, human beings often act in ways that are clearly contrary to what it means to be human.

We can deal with that problem by realizing all that exists consists of form and substance, what Aquinas called being and essence. Form or being consists of particular characteristics that, while they are part of the thing, and identify it as that particular member of a class, do not define it as itself.

Particular characteristics do not make up nature. Instead, the task facing a rational being is to bring particular characteristics (form) into conformity with nature (substance).

Take, for example, a red-haired human boy named Adam. His name, the redness of his hair, and other factors identify Adam as that particular boy, but they do not identify him as a boy. That depends on Adam having the characteristics of an immature human male.

Even that, however, does not get down to the fundamental question: what defines Adam as a human being first, and thus as a particular human being? Clearly it is not redness, or anything red would be human. Nor is it having hair, a name, or being male, or anything having hair, a name, or is male would be human, which we know is not the case.

Nor does changing one's physical characteristics alter essential human nature. A person does not become more fully human by dying his hair or altering his sex. To become more fully human, particular characteristics may be improved or corrected, but not turned into something else.

Manifestly, it is not having specific characteristics that defines a human being as human. This is despite the fact that the Supreme Court of the United States (evidently forgetting that "law is reason"[1]) has decided otherwise, as in *Roe v. Wade*.[2]

After much discussion that we need not go into here, Aristotle decided that it is the capacity for humanness that defines someone as human, not actually having humanness or any of its characteristics. Those who would deny the humanity of others or even of themselves

---

[1] Rommen, *The Natural Law, op. cit.,* 36.
[2] 410 U.S. 113 (1973).

because of some accidental characteristic therefore make a great error.[3]

Skin color, hair color, maleness, femaleness, sexual orientation, having or not having a name, stage of development, deformities, disabilities, social class, level of education, language, behavior, and so on — none of these or lack thereof define something as a human being. Christianity recognizes this: "There is neither Jew nor Greek: there is neither bond nor free: there is neither male nor female."[4] All these and an infinite number of other accidentals make no difference whether or not someone is human and therefore a person. They may affect what kind of person he is, but not the fact that he is a person.[5]

According to Aristotle, then, what defines someone as human is not actually *having* some or even all the characteristics of humanness. Rather, it is having the *capacity* to acquire and develop humanness. Personality — being a person — does not therefore depend on humanness, but on having the potential for humanness, in having a determinable instead of a determinate nature.

Aristotle, however, made a mistake, and ironically — man being the animal that reasons — violated his own first principle of reason to make it. This is important, because personalism is based on reason, so nothing involving the definition of person can contradict reason. That would invalidate the entire system.

To explain, the first principle of reason can be stated in two ways, one positive, one negative.

Positively, the first principle of reason is called the law of identity. That is, that which is true is as true, and is true in the same way, as everything else that is true.

For example, a rock is as much a rock as every other rock. It might be igneous, sedimentary, or metamorphic, but it is fully a rock. A semi-rock cannot exist, any more than someone can be a little bit dead. Furthermore, a rock is as truly a rock as a tree is as truly a tree, an animal is as truly an animal, or — and this is the point — as a human is as truly a human. Semi, partial, or incomplete humanity is out of the question.

---

[3] Aristotle called non-essential characteristics that something has that do not define it "accidentals" because it is only "by accident" that they exist. A human being, for example, is still human whether his hair is red or black, or he is bald.

[4] Gal. 3:28; cf. Col. 3:11, Rom. 3:22, 29.

[5] Reinforcing the natural law basis of the principle of human equality, Muhammad's "Farewell Sermon" following his performance of the Hajj, or pilgrimage to Mecca, makes a similar statement.

Negatively, the first principle of reason is called the law of (non) contradiction. That is, nothing can both "be" and "not be" at the same time under the same conditions.

For example, a rock cannot at the same time be a tree, nor a human be that which is not human. Most importantly, nothing can both exist and not exist at the same time.

Specifically, Aristotle's mistake was to assume that each human being has a different capacity for acquiring and developing human-ness. This, to him, explained why different people acquired different kinds and degrees of humanness, and why some people seemed to be only partly human, while others, although human in appearance, did not seem to be human in any degree. Such people could not become fully good, or good at all, due to the presumption that they could not develop a potential for humanity that they did not have.

Aquinas corrected Aristotle's mistake by realizing that — consistent with Aristotle's own principle of reason — the capacity to acquire and develop humanness could not be different for every human being, or it could not be what defines human beings as human beings. Instead, the capacity to become fully human, and human in the same way as all other humans, has to be "analogously complete" in everyone.

Aquinas's analogy of being does not mean "the same" or "identical." There are complex philosophical reasons why not, but they do not concern us for the purposes of this discussion. For our purposes, just think of "analogously complete" as meaning that all human beings have the same capacity to be fully human.

Good, therefore, is whatever is in conformity with nature. Evil is whatever is not in conformity with nature. That is why the natural law — the universal code of human behavior — can be summed up in the dictum, "Good is to be done, evil is to be avoided."

The Pursuit of Happiness

A better word for humanness is "virtue," defined as "the habit of doing good." Virtue is from the Latin and literally means "male-ness," but is construed in Thomist philosophy and thus in personalism as "human-ness."

All that exists aims at or seeks the good as the proper end or goal of existence, and the good consists of conforming to nature. It necessarily follows that for a human person, seeking the good means acquiring and developing habits of doing good, i.e., becoming virtuous or more fully human. That is how we link the end of human existence (seeking the good) to the pursuit of happiness.

In everyday speech, happiness is an emotion, "the satisfaction or contentment an individual feels in getting what is wanted."[6] That, however, is not the definition we want. Rather, what Jefferson referred to is a more philosophical meaning of happiness, something along the lines of Mortimer Adler's explanation:

> In its ethical or moral meaning, the word "happiness" refers to a life well lived, a whole life that is morally good because it is the product of virtue (or the habit of right desire) accompanied by the blessings of good fortune. . . .
> During one's life, one may be on the road to happiness, one may be described as *becoming* happy, but one cannot be said to be happy. Only when your life is over can someone else commenting on your life declare that you *had* lived a good life and can be described as a person who *had* achieved happiness.[7]

In other words, philosophically speaking, we cannot expect to achieve complete or full happiness in this life. We must, however, pursue happiness while alive, and strive to reach that goal by the end of our lives. This is consistent with the hope for a "happy death" of which the Church speaks, and it is what Jefferson meant.

As a side note, it is worthwhile to consider for a moment the tragedy of people who are convinced that they deserve happiness, rather than just the opportunity and means to attain happiness. Often confusing emotion and moral goodness, they spend their lives justifying anything and everything to get what they want in pursuit of the ephemeral satisfaction it brings.

Nor is the altruistic socialist or the philanthropic capitalist all that different from the selfish egoist in making this mistake. The socialist uses the coercive power of the State to force people to conform to his vision of the good — recall Robespierre and his "republican virtue" imposed with the guillotine.

In this, however, the socialist is in fundamental agreement with the capitalist who uses his personal wealth with respect to the end sought — the capitalist at least uses his own wealth to maintain a condition of dependency on others. Differing only in the degree of dependency imposed, both socialism and capitalism offend against the

---

[6] Mortimer J. Adler, *Adler's Philosophical Dictionary*. New York: Scribner, 1995, 104.
[7] *Ibid.*

dignity and self-determination of the human person by stripping most people of power, or being indifferent when others are powerless.

We are not born with virtue, but with the capacity to acquire and develop virtue. Nor can we be forced to be virtuous, for coercion takes away the virtuous character of an act. How, then, does someone pursue happiness, that is, become virtuous and conform himself to nature?

Ordinarily, we become virtuous by exercising our natural rights of life, liberty, and private property. This, however, must be in a manner consistent with the natural virtues of prudence (wisdom), temperance (self-control), fortitude (courage), and (above all) justice, fulfilled or completed by the supernatural virtues of faith, hope, and (above all) charity (love for others).

At first, of course, as children nothing is further from our minds than living the good life of virtue. Our parents, therefore, not only procreate us, but have the task of rearing us, that is, training us in virtue by teaching us right from wrong and helping us develop habits of doing good.

As we mature and demonstrate that we are able to exercise our natural rights in accordance with the virtues, our parents gradually grant us more power and control over our lives and give us more liberty. Finally, at our majority we are emancipated and take our places as members of society with the full exercise of all our rights.

Naturally, no one can expect to be perfectly human, except, in Christian belief, Jesus, the Second Person of the Blessed Trinity, Who is true God and true man, "true" here signifying "absolutely perfect." That is not what it means to become more fully human.

In Catholic belief, only God is perfect — infinitely perfect. In contrast, human beings are infinitely perfectible, and thus we can never achieve perfection. We can only come closer to perfection the more virtuous we become.

That is the theory, anyway. A serious problem in the modern world, however, is that a great many people have no real power to exercise their rights of life and liberty and are thereby inhibited from becoming virtuous. They are alienated from those institutions essential to maintaining personality, and often from the whole of society.

Exercising a right of any kind requires power and, as Daniel Webster (1782-1852) noted, "Power naturally and necessarily follows property." Power is the ability for doing, and a right is the power to do or not do some act in relation to others.

It follows that if someone has no power, he cannot exercise his rights, that is, act as a person. If he cannot exercise his rights, he cannot develop habits of doing good, *i.e.*, become virtuous. If he cannot become virtuous, he cannot pursue happiness and therefore does not conform to nature and fulfill the meaning and purpose of life. He is prevented or inhibited from becoming more fully human.

Most people in our highly technological world lack power over their own lives and liberty. This is because most people lack the economic power that derives from private property in capital. Capital ownership is the principal means by which people in an advanced economy can produce enough to become economically independent.

As a result, someone who owns no capital may be legally an adult, but socially and, especially, economically and politically, has little more power and independence than a child.[8] As a dependent on a private employer or on the State, he is to all intents and purposes a slave.[9]

The Common Good

One more element is essential if persons are to seek the good and become more fully human — a justly structured social order, that which embodies the common good of every human being. A just social order is so important that it is itself a preeminent good that must constantly be sought, protected, and perfected.

This is because the social order is the existing environment within which human beings as political animals ordinarily become virtuous, thereby becoming more fully human. As such, there is a built-in problem that is exacerbated by today's increasing powerlessness and alienation of the human person from productive activity and thus from participation in society.

Briefly, the social order, can be described as the concrete manifestation of how and to what extent every person within a society is able to access the common good. The common good as such consists of that vast network of institutions, "social tools" or "social habits" that, like individual rights, assist persons in becoming virtuous.

The distinction between the "common good" and the "social order" may be understood in terms of America's founding ideals as

---

[8] The ancient Roman law of the Twelve Tables made no real distinction between a man's children and his slaves. J.A. Crook, *Law and Life of Rome, 90 B.C.-A.D. 212.* Ithaca, New York: Cornell University Press., 1967, 55-57.

[9] *Rerum Novarum*, § 3.

institutionalized in the Declaration of Independence and the Constitution with the Bill of Rights, and how they were realized in the social order that existed at the time and through the present day. Basic human rights that should have been universally and equally accessible to every member of society were denied to specific classes of people such as women, people of African origin and Native Americans.

As a human construct, the common good is itself imperfect, being twice removed (so to speak) from what Catholics believe to be the Perfect Source, God. As a result, the common good and the social order are in a constant state of change and correction.

Both must therefore be monitored constantly to ensure that they are structured and functioning to assist people in becoming virtuous. If either the social order or the common good is materially flawed, people must organize and introduce changes into the system. Institutions may need to be restructured and new laws introduced so that the social order functions in a just way, enabling every person to pursue a life of virtue, help others and improve civilization.

While the capacity to acquire and develop virtue is common *sui generis* (generically, *i.e.*, by nature) to all human beings, how each person accesses the common good and pursues virtue is uniquely individual. My capacity to become virtuous, while no different than yours, is mine, and mine alone. I alone am responsible for the virtues and vices I acquire and develop of my own free will. Allowances can be made for environment, heredity, coercion or lack thereof, and many other factors, but ultimately each person is responsible for his own actions.

Because human beings are rational and ordinarily responsible for their own acts, something more is needed to bring persons together in solidarity than the individual capacity to become virtuous. We cannot count on instinct as other social animals do, on altruism toward others or enlightened self-interest to help us conform to our highest human nature, that is, to pursue happiness both as an individual and a member of a good society.

Instead, as political animals who are both individual and social, we have to organize and structure our social environment so as to maximize the exercise of our individual rights while respecting the rights of other persons. We work out and *institute* ways of doing things in a *systematic* way to help us meet our wants and needs in a consistent and effective, as well as just and virtuous, manner.

These "institutions" operating together are "the system." The system as a whole is the context within which human persons ordinarily realize their individual capacities for becoming virtuous in a social manner, that is, politically, within the *pólis* or structured community. The system — the social order — is therefore the concrete manifestation of the good common to all persons: the common good.

Understanding that the common good is not the aggregate of individual goods, or goods owned in common or by the State, or anything other than the institutional environment within which persons attain their individual goods, especially virtue, we realize just how serious is the problem of powerlessness and thus social alienation. As the common good is the environment within which persons ordinarily become virtuous and attain the good life, being alienated from it or lacking the power to gain full access to the institutions of the common good leads to individual and social degeneration.

Unless the common good is structured in a personalist way in all its aspects (that is, for the benefit, and in accordance with the nature of all persons), individual persons will suffer. Further, the social order degenerates to the point where it becomes anti-human and even antagonistic to the good life of virtue. Traditional Church (organized religion), State (civil society), and Family (marriage; domestic society), come under increasing attack, and attempts are made to abolish or overthrow a personalist understanding of these societies.

With the de-humanization of the unborn and the humanization of artificial persons such as corporations, the increasingly "virtual" nature of human interaction and growing dependency on the government, certain aspects of society are growing more anti-human, and at an accelerating pace. That this development has accompanied the alienation of persons from the common good by lack of power, opportunity, and access to the means of exercising their natural rights of life, liberty, and private property is a correlation too obvious to dismiss.

5
The Political Animal

In the previous chapter we examined the characteristics of what constitutes personality or personhood. We discovered that in practice, personalism consists of people conforming themselves to their own nature, thereby becoming more fully human by attaining an ever-greater degree of humanness or virtue.

We also discovered that the human person is both individual and social, what Aristotle termed a "political animal." A human being as a political animal is an individual, but more fully realizes his individuality within a consciously structured social environment wherein he gives of himself to others, becoming more himself in the process.

This is the common ground on which the social doctrine of Pius XI and the personalism of Wojtyła meet. Wojtyła's thought clarified what was implicit in that of Pius XI, just as Pius XI's breakthrough in moral philosophy built on the work of Leo XIII.

We now need to look in greater depth at three theories of personality that formed the modern world and how these are manifested in concepts of human dignity and sovereignty — in other words, *power*, who or what has it, and where it originates. That is, we need to examine the essence of personalism — the dignity and sovereignty of the human person — and why it matters where rights come from and who or what has them.

Rather than attempt a complete history or overview of political theory, we will limit our discussion to those theories of sovereignty behind socialism, capitalism, and economic personalism. These are, correspondingly, collectivism, individualism, and personalism.

Collectivism

Prior to and following the Reformation, stresses in society caused many people to begin questioning age-old assumptions about Church, State, and Family. Consistent with the emphasis of the reformers on faith instead of reason as the foundation of religious belief, old concepts of the human person that Scholastic philosophers such as Saint Thomas Aquinas had disproved or corrected surfaced once again. Of these, perhaps the most damaging was "the Divine Right of Kings."

Divine Right in its most extreme form was presented by Sir Robert Filmer (*cir.* 1588-1653), chief theologian of James VI/I (1566-1625) of

Scotland/England. This was in *Patriarcha, or, The Natural Power of Kings*, published posthumously in 1680, although the theory circulated in other forms prior to the book's publication.

According to Filmer, the only legitimate government is one that combines Church, State, and Family under a king appointed or sanctioned by God. This is supposedly because the king is directly descended from Adam, who in Filmer's interpretation of the Bible was given dominion over the entire Earth to the exclusion of all others.

In Filmer's theory, only the king has rights, because only the king is sovereign. All other people are limited to such rights as the king chooses to grant them. Rights may be revoked at the king's pleasure, although (being directly inspired by God and ruling in His Name), he will not do so unjustly.

Monsignor Ronald Arbuthnott Knox (1888-1957) noted the same strain of belief in his book, *Enthusiasm* (1950), which concentrated on the religious upheavals of the seventeenth and eighteenth centuries. Often used to justify various forms of Christian socialism, a constant theme among those whom Knox termed enthusiasts or ultrasupernaturalists is that the ungodly or those not specially chosen by God have no rights.[1]

Fittingly for socialists who sometimes place love of humanity above love of actual people, Knox defined enthusiasm as an "excess of charity [that] threatens unity."[2] Often accompanying this "excess of charity" is a deep suspicion of reason ("Man's miserable intellect"[3]), as well as of essential human nature unreformed by the vision of the enthusiast/socialist.[4]

Perhaps realizing the implications of the theory that in Christian belief all human beings are directly descended from Adam, Thomas Hobbes (1588-1679) substantially modified Filmer's concept. In *Leviathan, or, The Matter, Forme and Power of a Common-Wealth Ecclesiasticall and Civil* (1651, revised 1668), Hobbes's contribution to Divine Right theory was to claim that not the king *per se*, but the State itself is sovereign. Where Filmer's sovereign receives his power directly from God by right of his descent from Adam, Hobbes's sovereign receives its power from human beings via an irrevocable grant.

---

[1] Ronald A. Knox, *Enthusiasm: A Chapter in the History of Religion with Special Reference to the Seventeenth and Eighteenth Centuries*. New York: Oxford University Press, 1961, 3, 584.

[2] *Ibid.*, 1.

[3] *Ibid.*, 3, 578-580, 585-587.

[4] *Ibid.*, 3, 584-585.

Unlike Aristotle's "man as political animal" whose natural state is in society, Hobbes's concept of the state of nature is an anarchic chaos outside society. Desperate to gain the mutual protection of living in society, people come together and surrender their right to govern themselves to the sovereign, who may be either an individual or an "assembly of men." There is no recourse from any decision or act of the sovereign because by surrendering their rights, people have given their ultimate consent to everything.

By means of the sovereign gaining total control over life, liberty, and private property, the State becomes a "Mortall God" that rules on Earth as God rules in Heaven.[5] What began with Filmer as a Divine Right of Kings became in Hobbes's theory a Divine Right of the State.

It was not long, however, before Hobbes's theories, which he derived from Filmer, were themselves revised by others. One objection to Hobbes's version of consent theory is that, if people consent to surrender rights for themselves to enter society, what is to prevent people from taking them back again? Why is the grant irrevocable?

Further, even if the grant is irrevocable for the person who gave it originally, by what right does this bind his descendants? If people are born with rights, how can someone else surrender that which belongs to them, especially without their consent?

To get around this difficulty, later developments included the theory that God does not grant rights to actual human beings, but directly to the abstraction of humanity. The sovereign then decides which rights individuals should have, if any. Instead of persons creating the State by delegating rights to a government, the State creates persons by granting rights to human beings. Man is made for the State, not the State for man.

Although this is the theory of sovereignty embodied in all types of religious socialism, the error should be obvious. That is, if "God" is what Jews, Christians, and Muslims believe Him to be, then He cannot grant rights directly to humanity or any form of society. This is because "humanity" is a generalized concept, a creation of the human mind, and does not exist apart from the human minds that create it.

In the Abrahamic faiths, God is a perfect Being, and as such is omnipotent and omniscient. As a perfect Being, He does not deal in abstractions, which would be an indication of imperfection.

---

[5] Thomas Hobbes, *Leviathan*, II.xvii.

Abstractions are intellectual tools used by human beings because they cannot grasp the totality of knowledge of the Creator or of creation, and necessarily generalize or abstract.

Nor is the theory any sounder when the State or the collective replaces the Abrahamic God or Aristotle's conceptual "God of the Philosophers." The idea then becomes that the collective somehow self-generates rights which are then granted to people who come together to form society.

Again, the problem is that the collective is an abstraction, a thing, created by persons. Persons can delegate rights to a thing, but things cannot delegate rights to persons unless persons have delegated rights to the thing in the first place.

What came out of Divine Right theory, then, is the contradictory idea that natural rights are not inherent in the human person as part of nature, but in something that man himself creates. This is the source of the socialist principle that life, liberty, and — especially — private property can be taken away whenever it is deemed expedient or necessary by those in control of the collective.

French or European type liberal democracy is based on this principle. In its most extreme forms, the individual human person becomes irrelevant, or even a potential threat to the social order.

Individualism

Filmer's Divine Right theory did not go unchallenged, especially by the Catholic Church in the person of Roberto Francesco Romolo Cardinal Bellarmino, S.J. (1542-1621), Saint Robert Bellarmine. Bellarmine maintained that God creates every human being with natural rights, and thus with political sovereignty. As Filmer summarized the "vulgar opinion" of his chief opponent in the opening passage of *Patriarcha,*

> Mankind is naturally endowed and born with freedom from all subjection, and at liberty to choose what form of government it please, and that the power which any one man hath over others was at first bestowed according to the discretion of the multitude.[6]

In countering Filmer, Bellarmine influenced later political thought based on the concept of the sovereignty of the human person instead of an *élite* or a Divine Right monarch. He wrote extensively on the legitimacy, source, transmission, and application of the civil power,

---

[6] Sir Robert Filmer, *Patriarcha, or, The Natural Power of Kings,* I.i.

that is, of political sovereignty, especially in *De Laicis* and *De Summo Pontifice*.

Bellarmine contended that because the sovereign power resides in actual people, government only receives its power as a grant from human persons. In addition, distinguishing between political and social, he argued that the legitimacy of political power is demonstrated by the fact that it is necessary, man being social. Civil government would thus be required even if the Fall of Man had never occurred. As he explained,

> For even if servile subjection began after the sin of Adam, nevertheless there would have been political government even while man was in the state of innocence. And this is proved, firstly, because even then man would have been by nature a political and social animal, and hence would have had need of a ruler.[7]

Algernon Sidney (1623-1683) and John Locke (1632-1704) also challenged Filmer in *Discourses Concerning Government* (1698) and *Two Treatises on Government* (1690), respectively.[8] With some essential corrections from a personalist standpoint, the Founding Fathers of the United States used both Sidney and Locke.

Of these corrections, the most significant was the question whether man is by nature a political animal, or whether his natural state is outside society. Sidney and Locke assumed as a given that man's natural state is outside society.

In this both Sidney and Locke differed from Bellarmine, who accepted the opinion of Aristotle and Aquinas. That is, to Aristotle and Aquinas, man is by nature a political animal, subsiding naturally in a consciously structured social environment.

It is significant that both Locke and Sidney differed from Bellarmine on this point. At the same time, neither Locke nor Sidney appeared to realize that they had done so.

Locke's patron was the virulently anti-Catholic Anthony Ashley Cooper, First Earl of Shaftesbury (1621-1683).[9] Locke was therefore obliged to be hostile to Bellarmine, twisting the latter's theories into straw men that he ridiculed and demolished. He remained silent on the key point regarding whether man is naturally a member of

---

[7] *De Laicis*, Ch. VII.
[8] Sidney's book was published second, but it was written first.
[9] Shaftesbury was associated with the notorious Titus Oates and the "Popish Plot" (1678-1681) that resulted in the execution of at least fifteen innocent people, including Saint Oliver Plunkett (1625-1681).

society. This suggests Locke was either unaware of it or regarded it as unimportant.

For his part, Sidney expressed agreement with Bellarmine in everything except the latter's Catholic faith. Sidney would have found it essential to explain any other significant disagreement with Bellarmine in order to resolve the contradiction. Since Sidney did not mention any disagreement regarding whether or not man is by nature a political animal, it is reasonable to assume that he failed to realize there was a difference.

Failure to realize the difference or regard it as important was, not to exaggerate, a disaster. It was not enough to oppose the implicit collectivism of Hobbesian theory.[10] Guided by a theory not founded on the true nature of the human person led later political scientists to use Sidney and Locke to justify the development of an elitist theory of man as an individual, even solitary animal rather than a political animal.

In a startling paradox, the thought of Locke, Sidney, and others was integrated into that of Hobbes. This led to the formation of a uniquely English type of liberal democracy in which only an *élite* is considered effectively sovereign. It also set the stage for the development of social Darwinism in the nineteenth century.

Thus, while it is supremely contradictory, nineteenth century supporters of liberal democracy in England became at the same time ardent elitists. It comes as no surprise that Hobbes's thought was the starting point of the theory of political economy developed by Walter Bagehot (1826-1877), author of *The English Constitution* (1867) and *Lombard Street* (1873).

Bagehot's thesis in both his political and his economic thought was that sovereignty of the British Empire had passed from the hands of the monarchy and the aristocracy, to the House of Commons which represented people of wealth. According to Bagehot (who despised America and admired Hobbes), "The principle of popular government is that the supreme power, the determining efficacy in matters political, resides in the people — not necessarily or commonly in the whole

---

[10] Sidney and Locke wrote to refute Filmer, not Hobbes, but later political theorists compared the thought of Sidney and Locke to Hobbes, who had more influence than Filmer. Peter Laslett, Introduction to John Locke's *Two Treatises of Government*. Cambridge, U.K.: Cambridge University Press, 1960, 67-92.

people, in the numerical majority, but in a *chosen* people, a picked and selected people."[11]

John Maynard Keynes (1883-1946), principal author of the modern global economic system, relied heavily on Bagehot's thought in developing his own theories.[12] As a result, Keynesian economics is based on two profound errors. Both errors undermine the essential dignity and sovereignty of every human person by ignoring the ability of people to organize to reform the social order.

One, Keynes assumed as a given that the only way to finance new capital formation is to restrict consumption and accumulate the unconsumed production in the form of money savings. This tends to restrict ownership of most new capital to the already-wealthy, *i.e.*, those who can afford to divert a portion of their consumption incomes to fund investments. This creates the impression of a natural aristocracy of wealth destined to rule the rest of humanity.

As Keynes declared in *The Economic Consequences of the Peace* (1919), the book that established his reputation, "The immense accumulations of fixed capital which, to the great benefit of mankind, were built up during the half century before the war, could never have come about in a Society where wealth was divided equitably."[13]

Two, Keynes assumed — again as a given — that the State not only has the right and duty to regulate the currency, but to be the sole creator of money. As he asserted, the Absolutist State has the right to change unilaterally the terms of any agreement involving money, even "re-edit the dictionary" with respect to the definition of money.[14]

The Founding Personalists

In another one of those all-too-frequent paradoxes that obscure our understanding of personalism, Sidney and Locke were wrong when Bellarmine was right about man being a political animal, and right when Bellarmine was wrong about God not vesting any rights directly in the collective. Surprisingly, however, the American Founding Fathers managed to take the best of Sidney, Locke, and Bellarmine, and synthesize it into a theory of liberal democracy uniquely

---

[11] Walter Bagehot, *The English Constitution*. Brighton, UK: Sussex Academic Press, 1997, 17; cf. Knox, *Enthusiasm, op. cit.*, 584.

[12] John Maynard Keynes, "The Works of Bagehot," *The Economic Journal*, 25:369–375 (1915).

[13] John Maynard Keynes, *The Economic Consequences of the Peace* (1919), 2.iii.

[14] John Maynard Keynes, *A Treatise on Money, Volume I: The Pure Theory of Money.* New York: Harcourt, Brace and Company, 1930, 4.

American and at the same time (although we say this with some reservations), quintessentially Catholic.[15]

We say, "with some reservations," for to label any scientific theory, even in the social sciences as some do, "Catholic" is to misunderstand the respective roles of religious and civil society as well as of faith and of reason. At the same time it is accurate, if by "Catholic" we mean that a particular theory appears to conform to natural law principles as taught by the Catholic Church, which are, of course, not unique to the Church. The label "Catholic" must be understood in this context as universal or inclusive rather than exclusive.

Thus, Dr. Franz Hermann Mueller, a student of Father Heinrich Pesch, S.J., and member of the *Königswinterkreis* discussion group, noted as a serious error the failure among Catholics to distinguish between the natural and the supernatural in his Preface to Wilhelm Schwer's *Catholic Social Theory*.[16] As Mueller explained,

> [W]e still find the recurring confusion between morals and religion, between the order of nature and the order of grace. We find a tendency to fall into the opposite error of understanding the *causae secundae* and the role of nature. Especially among those who feel they must find a solution for social problems from the viewpoint of the *corpus Christi mysticum* alone. . . . [S]trictly speaking, it would be as incorrect to speak of Catholic sociology as to speak of Catholic economics.[17]

In any event, credit for the "Catholic" basis of the American Republic can probably be given to George Mason of Gunston Hall (1725-1792), sometimes called "the forgotten Founding Father." Most of the Founding Fathers got Bellarmine's thought secondhand through Locke and Sidney. Mason, however, may have read Bellarmine directly, imbibing a better understanding of natural law based on the Intellect, and thus developing a consistent theory of personalism.[18]

This is evident in how Mason, a slave owner, attempted to undermine the legal justification for slavery when he drafted the Virginia Declaration of Rights in 1776.

When the Virginia Convention met in the Spring of that year, they adopted a resolution to prepare a declaration of fundamental natural rights. As the most experienced legal writer in Virginia, Mason drafted the document. Following his usual practice, he included a

---

[15] See de Tocqueville, *Democracy in America, op. cit.*, I.xvii, II.vi.

[16] Rev. Wilhelm Schwer, *Catholic Social Theory*. Saint Louis, Missouri: B. Herder Book Company, 1940.

[17] *Ibid.*, vi-vii.

[18] Rager, *The Political Philosophy of St. Robert Bellarmine, op. cit.*, 83-90.

provision that implicitly destroyed the legal justification of chattel slavery by including all human beings without qualification:

> That all men are by nature equally free and independent, and have certain inherent rights, of which they cannot, by any compact, deprive or divest their posterity; namely, the enjoyment of life and liberty, with the means of acquiring and possessing property, and pursuing and obtaining happiness and safety.

If *all* men are naturally members of society, regardless of circumstances, it logically follows that this applies to slaves. The clear implication is that slaves, as human beings and thus persons, have the natural right to be free.

Unfortunately, the conservative ("aristocratic") delegates to the Virginia Convention were ready for Mason. They immediately challenged the language, accusing Mason (with justification) of wanting to abolish slavery.[19]

Mason was forced to amend the language, or he faced the possibility of losing Virginia's support for the Revolution. As historian Robert Rutland noted,

> As finally approved, the first sentence read "That all men are by nature equally free and independent, and have certain inherent rights, of which, *when they enter into a state of society*, they cannot, by any compact, deprive or divest their posterity; . . ." The italicized phrase, with its implicit proposition that slaves are not members of society, placated the opposition.[20]

Possibly warned by Mason's experience, Thomas Jefferson was able to retain the basis of natural law and inalienable rights in the Declaration of Independence adopted a month later. This, however, was only at the cost of surrendering a passage condemning slavery and leaving out mention of private property as a natural right.

Still, a Bill of Rights was added to the 1789 Constitution[21] that included recognition of private property in the takings clause of the Fifth Amendment. More to the point, the personalist orientation of the document is stated in the Preamble: "We, the People," with the clear implication that the State only gets what rights it has from actual human beings who are, *ipso facto*, persons with inalienable rights. When Pope Pius IX promulgated a constitution for the Papal

[19] Robert A. Rutland, *George Mason: Reluctant Statesman*. Baton Rouge, Louisiana: Louisiana State University Press, 1961, 51-53; Florette Henri, *George Mason of Virginia*. New York: Crowell-Collier Press, 1971, 93.

[20] Rutland, *op. cit.*, 54.

[21] Demanded by Mason, rejected by James Madison, then reintroduced by Madison.

States, "the Fundamental Statute,"[22] it was modeled on the U.S. Constitution, for which he had high regard.[23]

Particularly after the invention of the cotton gin made growing cotton inordinately profitable,[24] however, efforts to preserve and extend slavery dictated U.S. policy at home and abroad.[25] At the same time, demands for the abolition of "the peculiar institution" that violated the essential dignity and rights of human beings became more insistent as its continued existence became intolerable.

Constitutionally speaking, matters came to a head in 1857 with the notorious Dred Scott case.[26] The U.S. Supreme Court overturned the decision of the Missouri Supreme Court granting a slave, Dred Scott, his freedom. In so doing the Court completely changed the political philosophy of the United States and the basis of the Constitution.[27]

According to the opinion rendered by Chief Justice Roger Brooke Taney (1777-1864), rights are a grant from the State to people, not from the people to the State. Under Taney's ruling, the State creates persons by deciding who has rights; persons (who in the view of America's founders have rights by nature) do not create the State. Socialist political theory was used to justify agrarian capitalism.

Following the American Civil War (1861-1865), the Fourteenth Amendment was adopted in part to overturn *Scott v. Sandford* and restore the personalist basis of the Constitution. In 1873, however, in what constitutional scholar William Winslow Crosskey (1894-1968) described as a power grab by the Supreme Court, the Fourteenth Amendment was nullified in the opinion of the *Slaughterhouse Cases*.[28] This created the precedent for *Roe v. Wade* and similar decisions.

The shift in political philosophy probably would have failed to take root had it not been for one factor. By the final decade of the

---

[22] "Pius IX and the Revolutions at Rome," *The North American Review*, Vol. 74, No. 154, January 1852.

[23] Rommen, *The State in Catholic Thought, op. cit.*, 481, 605.

[24] From 1803 to 1937 cotton was the single largest U.S. export. See the importance of technology as a "lever of change," pp. 122-124.

[25] See David Christy, *Cotton is King, or, The Culture of Cotton, and its Relation to Agriculture, Manufactures and Commerce; to the Free Colored People; and to Those Who Hold that Slavery is In Itself Sinful; by an American*. Cincinnati, Ohio: Moore, Wilstach, Keys, 1855.

[26] *Scott v. Sandford*, 60 U.S. 393 (1857).

[27] William W. Crosskey, *Politics and the Constitution in the History of the United States*. Chicago, Illinois: The University of Chicago Press, 1953, 1089.

[28] Crosskey, *Politics and the Constitution, op. cit.*, 1130.

nineteenth century the United States had begun its rapid shift from a widespread ownership economy promoting opportunity, independence and the rights, powers and responsibilities of the individual, to the wage system of an industrialized economy that turned the mass of human beings into human resources.[29] The end of free land, as historian Frederick Jackson Turner (1861-1932) declared in his "frontier thesis," meant the end of the uniquely American form of liberal democracy.[30]

Fortunately, Pius XI in his social doctrine recognized the need for a political theory consistent with the nature of social justice as a particular virtue, and that is based on the dignity and sovereignty of the human person under God. This he found in the political philosophy of Bellarmine as corrected by the American Founding Fathers.

In short order Pius XI beatified Bellarmine (1923), issued the encyclical *Quas Primas* (1925) in part to promulgate and commemorate his correction of Bellarmine's political philosophy, canonized Bellarmine (1930), and named him a "Doctor of the Church" (1931). Earlier in 1931 he had issued *Quadragesimo Anno* to present the first part of his social doctrine, followed by the second part in *Divini Redemptoris* (1937).

As we noted in Chapter 2, however, there was a serious omission from Pius XI's social program. Sound as an application of doctrine, it still did not include a financially feasible and morally acceptable means whereby ordinary people could acquire and possess private property in capital without redistributing wealth or savings from the "haves" to the "have nots."

Saving the necessary amount of money by restricting consumption — the suggested method — is usually not practical for most people, especially if they are poor. On the scale of an entire economy it reduces consumption to the point where new capital formation is also reduced. As a result, due to lack of demand for capital, there could easily be insufficient capital available for everyone to be able to own unless supplemented with redistribution.

And, as we will see in the next chapter, without expanded capital ownership, it becomes virtually impossible to implement Catholic social teaching without falling into injustice and offending against human dignity.

---

[29] *Quadragesimo Anno*, § 135.
[30] Frederick Jackson Turner, "XVIII. — The Significance of the Frontier in American History," *Annual Report of the American Historical Association for the Year 1893*. Washington, DC: Government Printing Office, 1894, 200.

6
Sacred and Inviolable

As presented in the thought of Pope Pius XI and explained by Father William J. Ferree, the act of social justice requires recognition and protection of three natural rights of the human person. These are life, liberty, and private property.

Every human being's right to life should be self-evident, although it has been called into question today. This is a result of the Culture of Death, a social environment generally contrary to human nature that does not value human life, or that values human life for reasons other than as an end in itself. The rise of the Culture of Death is a development directly related to the general powerlessness of the great mass of people and the rise to power of an economic and political *élite* that controls the whole of life insofar as it is able.

Liberty — including freedom of association and contract — is another self-evident truth, especially in Pius XI's social doctrine.[1] Social justice is a particular virtue, a habit carried out by human beings, requiring voluntary action directed at the common good, and whose distinguishing characteristic is organization. Without liberty, persons are unable to organize for the common good except at the risk of their lives or property.

Social justice does not operate in a vacuum, nor is it simply an esoteric concept with no relevance to the real world or everyday life. To understand the relevance of social justice to our daily lives, however, we need to understand a critical mechanism that enables us to exercise and defend our liberty — private property in productive things (capital).

What is Private Property?

Almost nothing in economics, finance, and political economy is more misunderstood than private property. The sole exception is money and credit, which are simply two different forms of the same thing: promises and the keeping of promises.[2] Furthermore, private property and money are inextricably linked.[3]

---

[1] *Quadragesimo Anno*, §§ 24-25, 35, 50, 86-88, 92, 95, 97, 109-110.

[2] "Money and Credit are essentially of the same nature; Money being only the highest and most general form of Credit." Henry Dunning Macleod, *The Theory of Credit*. Longmans, Green and Co., 1894, 82.

[3] Irving Fisher, *The Purchasing Power of Money*. New York: Macmillan, 1931, 4-6.

Much of the misunderstanding regarding private property comes from the fact that many people have no real idea of what property consists, nor even what is (or is not) private property. They tend to think of property as that which is owned, such as land or a tractor. As a result, they confuse each person's natural right to be an owner (which is inclusive) with the rights that an owner has in the thing owned and how what is owned can be used (which is exclusive).

This distinction seems trivial and even meaningless to people who confuse the right *to* property and the rights *of* property. This leads to misunderstanding the natural rights that define each human being as a natural person, and it undermines the foundation of Catholic social teaching.

To clarify, property is not the thing that is owned. Rather, property is both the right to be an owner (to have access, *i.e.,* "dominion"), as well as the bundle of rights of control and the fruits or profits that define what an owner may do with the things that he owns; what legitimate and non-harmful ends their uses may be directed, *i.e.,* "destination") and what natural resources, wealth-producing technologies, patents, and other non-human inputs to the productive process a person can own.

Under the name "generic right of dominion" the Catholic Church recognizes that the right to be an owner is inherent and absolute, that is, without restriction, exception, or qualification, in every child, woman, and man. The right to property is part of human nature itself, an integral aspect of that capacity to become virtuous that defines us as human beings.

This is because taking away the right to be an owner redefines a being as no longer human, or as human in a way different from other humans. Asserting that some humans are not human, or that they are human in a different way than other humans, violates the first principle of reason and offends against human dignity and the common good at the deepest level.

Complementing the absolute right to be an owner is what the Catholic Church calls "the universal destination of all goods." In contrast to the natural right to be an owner, the socially determined bundle of rights that define how an owner may use what is owned is necessarily limited, or society would dissolve in chaos.

As with the exercise of political power in a democracy, with the exercise of private property there is a fundamental tension — balancing private, individual rights with the needs of other individuals and groups, and the demands of the common good. That is why Bellarmine in his political philosophy rejected the belief of the Fraticelli and others that man before the Fall and living in full conformity with God's Will would have no need of government or of private property.

Thus, the universal destination of all goods means that no one may exercise property in any way that harms one's self, other individuals or groups, or the common good as a whole. This last, a demand of social justice, does not mean that private property is abolished. Nor does it mean that private property is allowed only as an expedient or out of necessity.

It means, rather, that at the very least an owner should not harm the legitimate interests and rights of others. In pursuing his own interests, each person should exercise his private property rights in ways that indirectly benefit (or at least cause no harm to) the whole of society. Stewardship, a one-word term for the universal destination of all goods, is a principle guiding use, not a transfer of ownership to the community.

A proper understanding of the relationship between the generic right of dominion and the universal destination of all goods nullifies the arguments of both capitalists and socialists. Socialists cannot claim that the meaning of the universal destination of all goods vests ultimate ownership in the community or humanity, for that contradicts the generic right of dominion. Capitalists cannot claim that the absolute right to be an owner (the generic right of dominion) gives them the unlimited or monopolistic right to accumulate wealth or the right to act without restraint when using their goods, for that contradicts the universal destination of all goods.

Thus, "property" includes both an absolute, inclusive aspect, and a limited, exclusive aspect. Politics consists of properly structuring institutions to provide equality of opportunity and means to exercise the rights of life, liberty, and private property, and providing for exceptions when warranted for the common good and (in extreme cases) individual good.[4] Social justice consists of maintaining and reforming institutions to design and provide the proper social environment within which all people can exercise their rights and thereby become virtuous.

In theory, everything can be privately owned. It may, however, be expedient at times to limit what as well as how much can be owned.

---

[4] *Rerum Novarum*, § 22.

Most people would agree, for instance, that (aside from the issue of their moral legitimacy) weapons of mass destruction should not be owned privately.

Furthermore, as articulated by Louis Kelso and Mortimer Adler in their principle of limitation, no one should be able to use his property in ways that prevent other people from acquiring productive capital or exercising property rights. [5] (Today we are beginning to see the economic and political consequences of a system that enables a small class of owners or the State to gain a virtual monopoly of ownership and control over ever-advancing technologies that are producing a greater and greater proportion of goods and services, while eliminating the need for human labor, the only way most people earn a living.)

It may also be appropriate at times to limit the ways in which something may be privately owned. Such possessions as land and natural resources, for example, being finite and created without human input, may call for different forms of private ownership than man-made capital.

Technology and other man-made forms of productive capital are constantly being created. It becomes possible for every person to own a share of newly created capital, individually or jointly in free association with others. There is, however, not enough land and natural resources for everyone to have an exclusive ownership stake as a sole proprietor. In that case, instead of mandating public ownership — which abolishes private property — it would be more consistent with a personalist orientation to make land and natural resources jointly owned by everyone in the community.

In the case of "joint ownership," every person could have a defined private property stake by owning a share of the whole, without necessarily identifying which part of the whole belongs to each person. Corporations and cooperatives are owned in this manner, as were the so-called Commons, with each resident having the defined right to, e.g., graze a certain number of animals or gather a certain amount of fuel.

Why Private Property?

The institution of private property in capital is an essential component of a justly structured social order. This has been recognized from the earliest times, from the Biblical vine and fig tree,[6] Aristotle's

---

[5] Kelso and Adler, *The Capitalist Manifesto, op. cit.,* 68.
[6] Mic. 4:4; 1 Kings 4:25; Zech. 3:10.

acknowledgment that property is essential for households and thus for a stable *pólis*,[7] and the Gracchi agitation for redistribution of common lands[8] illegally converted to private property by the rich,[9] to give a few examples.

That Catholic social teaching assumes a central role for widespread private ownership of capital astonishes even many Catholics. They refer to sections in the encyclicals that in their opinion change or (more fairly) correct the accepted secular interpretation of private property, bringing it into conformity with their understanding of the law of the Gospels.

More to the point, they cite passages in Scripture that — they claim — support their position. There is, for example, the incident of the rich young man who comes to Jesus and asks what he must do to be saved.[10]

Jesus tells the young man to keep the Commandments. This the young man says he has done from his youth, but wants to know what more can he do?

That is when Jesus tells him to go and sell all that he has, give the proceeds to the poor, and come and follow Him. Being troubled by this (for he is very wealthy), the young man goes away.

At that point Jesus remarks that it is easier for a camel to go through the eye of a needle than for a rich man to enter the Kingdom of Heaven. Surprised, for the rich were presumably favored by God, the disciples ask how, then, can *anyone* be saved?

Far from being a condemnation of wealth, the incident of the rich young man actually reminds us that wealth is good. Reading the passage carefully, we realize that Jesus did not demand the surrender of wealth in order to be saved.

If that were so, then Jesus lied to the young man when He said all that is necessary is to keep the Commandments. It is only when the young man asks what *more* can he do that Jesus tells him to give away his possessions.

---

[7] *Politics*, 1253b23.
[8] These were not the same as the Commons of the Middle Ages and later, but state-owned lands apportioned to private use to ensure that every family (in theory at least) had a capital asset to support the status of Roman citizen.
[9] Plutarch, "Life of Tiberius Gracchus," *Lives of the Noble Grecians and Romans*. New York, Modern Library, (ND), 998-1007; "Life of Gaius Gracchus," *ibid.*, 1010.
[10] Mt. 19:23-26; Mk. 10:24-27; Lk. 18:24-27.

As the Church has taught from the beginning, giving up worldly goods — and keep in mind that they are goods, not evils — is a "counsel of perfection." We can be saved by keeping the Commandments, but if we want to simplify matters, we should rid ourselves of earthly distractions and focus only on God:

> Come to me all you that labor and are burdened, and I will refresh you. Take up my yoke upon you, and learn of me, because I am meek, and humble of heart: And you shall find rest to your souls. For my yoke is sweet and my burden light.[11]

While it is related in the Acts of the Apostles that some of the early Christians held their goods in common, the private ownership of wealth is never condemned.[12] Correlation with other passages clearly indicates that not everyone sold his goods and donated the proceeds to the common fund. It was purely voluntary. Ananias and Sapphira were condemned not for retaining some of their wealth, but for lying about it.[13]

It is, however, in the Parable of the Talents that we see the importance of private property in capital for living a virtuous life.[14]

The message of the parable is obvious: we are to use the gifts God gives us properly. Specifics of the story, however, seem a little contrived, even artificial. This impression strengthens when we look into the original language.

A man preparing to go on a journey calls in three slaves — yes, *slaves*, not servants or employees. To one he hands over five talents, or 30,000 drachma, a drachm being a good day's wages. To the other two he hands over two talents and one talent, respectively.

When the man returns from his journey, he demands an accounting of the enormous sums of money he had handed over. The two slaves who had received five talents and two talents doubled the money. They are manumitted and given ownership of the cash.

The slave who received one talent buried it and made no profit at all. His master takes back the money and hands it over to the former slave who had started with five talents. The worthless wretch who buried the money instead of investing it remains a slave.

The story as a story, incomprehensible to modern listeners, would have made perfect sense to Jesus's audience. In the Roman world, the

---

[11] Mt. 11:28-30.
[12] Acts 2:44-45.
[13] Acts 5:1-11.
[14] Mt. 25:14-30; Lk. 19:12-27.

justification for slavery was that someone was a criminal or otherwise incapable of taking care of himself without a master.

Manumission of slaves was not uncommon in Roman society, which actually caused labor shortages when slave owners took their responsibilities seriously. A master's job was to prepare both his children and his slaves (considered the same under the Law of the Twelve Tables) to take their places in Roman society as virtuous adults, which they could not do if children remained infants or slaves were kept in bondage.

To the Roman way of thinking, the best way to prepare children and slaves to grow in virtue, develop as persons, and enter society was to train them to manage property. A sum of money or other wealth called a *peculium* would be put in a slave's custody, and he was free to do with it as he wished, unless his master, the real owner, had given him other instructions (which was rare).[15]

It was not unusual at the conclusion of a successful venture or career for the slave to receive not only his freedom, but the entire amount of the *peculium*, all the profits, and even Roman citizenship. Jesus's listeners would not have been confused in the least by the story, although they might have shaken their heads in wonder at the stupidity of the slave who failed to take advantage of the opportunity he had been given.

Power and Private Property

Nor does widespread private property in capital only relate to the individual level of the common good. Accounting for the central role it plays in Catholic social teaching, it has important social aspects as well.

As far as Aristotle was concerned, for example, a free man without capital ownership was a "masterless slave," a nobody; even a slave had more status as a possession than a free man had as a non-owner. One of the more remarkable features of Jesus's earthly ministry was to treat non-owning wage workers as if they were as much persons and full members of society as owners — which, of course, they were and are, but without effective means of realizing their status.

As we saw in Chapter 4, full participation in society and the status of person require that someone be able to exercise the rights that

---

[15] Crook, *Law and Life of Rome, op. cit.,* 54, 56, 63, 110-11, 129, 188-189, 241; K. R. Bradley, *Slaves and Masters in the Roman Empire: A Study in Social Control.* Oxford, U.K.: Oxford University Press, 1984, 108-110.

define him as a person. Exercise of rights requires power, and power follows property.

In an advanced economy when people have only their labor to sell, those without private property in capital are at an extreme disadvantage when it comes to exercising their rights. They must always take into consideration whoever or whatever provides them with their subsistence, whether it be a private employer or the State. Displeasing whoever controls your subsistence is the short road to destitution for you and your dependents.

Nor does this change even if employers are generous or the State mandates certain benefits. By imposing and maintaining dependency on others, those in power, whether they are of a private sector *élite* or a public sector bureaucracy, will maintain control to retain power and gain desired ends.

This ranges from a private sector employer threatening to close a factory if worker demands become too great, to a politician claiming that government benefits will be reduced or eliminated by his political opponents if he is not returned to office. In contrast, as capital owners receiving independent capital incomes, people can decide where to work (or even whether to work), and for whom to vote without having to consider how they will afford their next meal.

The social importance of widespread capital ownership comes into even sharper focus when we consider the economic system, accurately if briefly described as the production, distribution, and consumption of marketable goods and services. Where the status of person and the maintenance of a politically just society can only be supported by a broad diffusion of political power through equal access to the ballot, the capacity to consume and the maintenance of an economically just society can only be supported by the widespread opportunity and ability to produce through one's capital as well as one's labor.

Lack of capital ownership is not usually too much of a problem when human labor is the predominant means of production. Except for anyone unjustly enslaved, everyone owns human labor simply because he is human. Further, human labor is inseparable from human beings. Respect for the dignity of the human person naturally commands respect for human labor.

The picture changes when land ownership is concentrated or technology advances. The non-owning worker is at a disadvantage when few people own land, or when labor is displaced by more efficient machinery. In both instances he is cut off from the means of being productive and thus of securing personal power. Without power, he loses control over his life and that of his dependents.

The system is thrown out of balance when any significant number of people are unable to produce what they need to consume. This is so whether they produce directly for their own consumption, or indirectly by exchanging what they produce for what others produce. As a result, a relatively few people produce far more than they can possibly consume, while the vast majority are unable to consume all that others produce.

Unless a means is found to make as many people as possible capital owners and thus producers without harming existing owners, wealth will become increasingly concentrated. It is not by chance that a tiny group of extraordinarily wealthy people today own more net wealth than half the world's population combined.[16]

A truly personalist society is impossible without widespread capital ownership, as the popes have acknowledged. Without the political power that accompanies capital ownership, people are alienated from the life of the citizen in the State and become effective slaves, either of private employers or of State bureaucrats.

Without people having the economic power that accompanies capital ownership, the State itself is endangered through the failure of the economy that gives life to the body politic. For both individual and social reasons, then, Pius XI declared,

> The redemption of the non-owning workers — this is the goal that Our Predecessor [Leo XIII] declared must necessarily be sought. And the point is the more emphatically to be asserted and more insistently repeated because the commands of the Pontiff, salutary as they are, have not infrequently been consigned to oblivion either because they were deliberately suppressed by silence or thought impracticable although they both can and ought to be put into effect. . . . [T]he number of the non-owning working poor has increased enormously and their groans cry to God from the earth. Added to them is the huge army of rural wage workers, pushed to the lowest level of existence and deprived of all hope of ever acquiring "some property in land," and, therefore, permanently bound to the status of non-owning worker unless suitable and effective remedies are applied.[17]

---

[16] See the October 2018 Credit Suisse Research Institute, *Global Wealth Report 2018*, credit-suisse.com. Note that this refers to *net* worth; many people in the developed world with high incomes have negative net worth due to a large burden of consumer and other non-productive debt.

[17] *Quadragesimo Anno*, § 59.

7
The Economics of Reality and Justice

Mystifying people who confuse the means by which a goal is attained with the goal itself, both Leo XIII and Pius XI made widespread capital ownership, which empowers people, the cornerstone of their social program. This follows from the cornerstone of their social doctrine, which is respect for the dignity of the human person, which requires empowerment.

Respect for human dignity entails something more than guaranteeing material needs and humane treatment. That is what the socialists demand and assume is the goal of Catholic social teaching.

A relatively minor issue is whether it is even possible for some authority, individual, or group to assess the needs of others in an accurate or even meaningful manner. For example, people require food, but the amount and kind can differ greatly among individuals.

As Dr. Leo Alexander (1905-1985) noted in his article, "Medical Science Under Dictatorship,"[1] the practice of medicine (and, by extension, anything else) in accordance with political considerations is an essential adjunct to tyranny. When "the People" (an abstraction) displaces actual people as the object of concern, personal power disappears and all true respect for human dignity is lost.

It may sound trite, but the end does not justify the means, especially for beings with a higher destiny than mere animal existence. Saint-Simon's socialist principle that the end justifies the means to improve the standard of living for the poor is no more valid under natural law than the *laissez-faire* capitalist principle that all that exists must be subordinated to increasing profits and the accumulation of wealth.

Why Binary Economics?

In all forms of tyranny, the State or community dictates what people must do and how they must do it instead of maintaining the *pólis* so that people can pursue their own destinies within established parameters as they themselves see fit. When most people lack private property in capital and thus lack power, however, they often have no

---

[1] Leo Alexander, "Medical Science under Dictatorship," *New England Journal of Medicine.* 241 (2): 39–47.

choice but to comply with the wishes of those who do have property, whether they are a private sector capitalist *élite* or a socialist bureaucracy.

Louis Kelso, a corporate finance lawyer and personalist economist, began seeking a solution to the problem of powerlessness and social alienation when during the Great Depression of the 1930s he saw unemployed men illegally riding freight trains in an often fruitless search for jobs. Kelso was struck by the paradox of widespread unemployment and want in a country with tremendous productive capacity. This alerted him to the fact that something was fundamentally wrong with the economic system.

After studying the problem, Kelso realized that as technology advanced, consumers had become (to use our term, not Kelso's) alienated from the ability to produce with labor alone. At the same time, capital owners were producing far more than they could consume with the income generated by their capital.

More efficient machinery had largely displaced human labor as the predominant factor of production. As a result, owners of labor (workers) could not produce enough with their labor to exchange for what owners of capital produced with their technology.

Paradoxically, what seemed like excess aggregate supply and inadequate aggregate demand was really a problem of grossly unequal productive power and thus effective demand concentrated in too few hands. As Jean-Baptiste Say (1767-1832) concluded when explaining his "Law of Markets" (below) to the Reverend Thomas Malthus (1766-1834),

> I had said, "As each of us can only purchase the productions of others with his own productions — as the value we can buy is equal to the value we can produce — the more men can produce, the more they will purchase." Thence follows the other conclusion, which you refuse to admit: "that if certain goods remain unsold, it is because other goods are not produced, and that it is production alone which opens markets to produce."[2]

With the value of their labor falling relative to technology as the productiveness of capital far outstripped that of labor, workers increasingly relied on union pressure and government coercion to redistribute capital ownership income to keep the economy running. The rise of the Welfare/Servile State increased the problem.

---

[2] Jean-Baptiste Say, *Letters to Malthus*. London: Sherwood, Neely, and Jones, 1821, 3.

Later, in the books he co-authored with Mortimer Adler,[3] Kelso noted that the economic alienation he observed was only part of a much larger problem. Expanded capital ownership is important not merely for income, but as a key element in a free and just society; political democracy requires economic democracy.

Discovering what in the economic system caused the inability of people to be productive and thus unable to generate sufficient purchasing power, however, was Kelso's primary focus. At the heart of what he eventually called "binary economics" is the realization that capital and labor are both productive, and they are both productive (*i.e.*, produce goods and services) in the same way. Defining labor as all human inputs to production, and capital (including land) as all non-human inputs, Kelso recognized labor and capital as two interdependent yet distinct factors of production.

Kelso's analysis came into conflict with prevailing economic theory and political policy that recognizes only labor as productive. Mainstream economics claims that capital at best only enhances labor productivity, defining "productivity" as "output per labor hour." This leads to the logical absurdity that labor is infinitely productive at the point where it has been completely removed from the production process, *e.g.*, self-service elevators or automated factories.

As Kelso reasoned, when the productiveness of one factor falls relative to the other factor — as labor does relative to capital when technology advances — owners of labor must replace the decline in their labor productivity by becoming owners of capital. Similarly, if in the unlikely event capital productiveness were to fall relative to that of labor, owners of capital would have to replace the productiveness of capital with that of labor, preferably their own.

Kelso and the popes came to the same conclusion from opposite ends of the question. The popes began with the problem of social alienation and realized that reconnecting the human person to society requires the power of widespread capital ownership that would also solve the problem of the growing wealth and income gap caused by the inability to produce sufficiently. Kelso began with the problem of the growing wealth and income gap caused by the inability to produce and realized that reconnecting the human person to the process of production through expanded capital ownership would also reconnect the human person to society.

---

[3] *The Capitalist Manifesto* (1958) and *The New Capitalists* (1961).

Nor were the popes and Kelso the first to realize the importance of expanded capital ownership for a just society or workable economy. William Cobbett (1763-1835), the English Radical politician and journalist, insisted with Aristotle and Adler that the propertyless condition is tantamount to slavery. As he declared in his best-known work, *A History of the Protestant Reformation in England and Ireland* (1827),

> Freedom is not an empty sound; it is not an abstract idea; it is not a thing that nobody can feel. It means, — and it means nothing else, — the full and quiet enjoyment of your own property. If you have not this, if this be not well secured to you, you may call yourself what you will, but you are a slave.[4]

At the other end of the political spectrum, the English investment banker Charles Morrison argued in his book, *An Essay on the Relations Between Labour and Capital* (1854), that propertyless wage workers must become part owners of the businesses that employed them. This would ensure that they had adequate income, whether through dividends or profit sharing.

English corporations in Morrison's day, however, did not enjoy limited liability except by special act of Parliament. Further, any participation in management or profits was deemed "ownership" under the English law of partnerships. That made anyone who received anything other than a fixed wage jointly and severally liable for all debts of the corporation. Workers who participated in ownership could lose everything they owned and go to prison if the corporation failed to pay its debts.[5]

Morrison's book was instrumental in persuading Parliament to pass the Limited Liability Act 1855.[6] This made it possible for ordinary people to participate in ownership — if they could save enough to purchase shares. Most could not, even when shares were available.

Having arrived in the same place — the need for expanded capital ownership — the question for Kelso became the same one the popes had failed to address adequately: how to achieve the desired goal. Redistribution of existing capital, whether voluntarily through

---

[4] William Cobbett, *A History of the Protestant Reformation in England and Ireland* (1827), §456.
[5] Imprisonment for debt is still possible in Great Britain, although a number of reforms have been instituted, beginning with the Debtor's Act 1869, 32 & 33 Vic., c. 62.
[6] 18 & 19 Vict c 133.

philanthropy[7] or (more likely) involuntarily through what the socialists incorrectly called distributive justice would destroy that which
they were claiming to restore by keeping people dependent.

On the other hand, attempting to finance expanded capital ownership by reducing one's consumption and accumulating savings (the
specific suggestion advanced by the popes) is not merely inadequate,
but impossible for most people. Not only are most people unable to
save in appreciable amounts, the required diminution in mass consumption even if they could save would render new capital formation
a bad investment. There is, after all, no reason to invest in additional
capital when there is insufficient demand for what is already being
produced.

Solving the Problems

In his 1936 *Essay on the Restoration of Property*, Hilaire Belloc
identified five points that had to be addressed if widespread capital
ownership was to be restored as a distinguishing characteristic of society. These were,

- **Concentrated Corporate Ownership,**
- **Money and Credit,**
- **Taxation,**
- **Retail Distribution, and**
- **Sustainability of Initial Efforts.**

Belloc's identification of key points was accurate, as was his statement of the problem. His proposed solutions were grossly inadequate,
however, leading him to conclude that the goal he sought was virtually impossible to achieve.[8]

Kelso's solutions as developed and refined by the interfaith Center
for Economic and Social Justice (CESJ) not only address Belloc's
points, but are based on techniques applying the three principles of
economic justice. As systematized by Kelso and Adler in their 1958
collaboration, *The Capitalist Manifesto*, and developed and refined by
CESJ (which expanded Kelso and Adler's "principle of limitation" to
the concept of "social justice"), the tripartite principles of economic
justice are,

---

[7] Philanthropists usually ignore the need for widespread capital ownership and redistribute wealth in ways that keeps people dependent.

[8] Belloc, *The Restoration of Property, op. cit.*, 10-11.

- **Participative Justice,** or the input principle, "from each according to his productive contributions through his labor and capital,"[9]

- **Distributive Justice,** or the out-take principle, "to each according to his labor and capital contributions,"[10] and

- **Social Justice,** or the feedback and corrective principle that repairs the institutional environment whenever anyone is denied equal opportunity to contribute to production through his labor and/or capital, or from receiving his just due according to his contributions.

As is clear from the previous chapters in this book where they were covered in a general way, all three principles are based solidly on the natural law. They will be explained in more depth in the next chapter to demonstrate their application to binary economics and to economic personalism. At this point, however, we are interested in program specifics that when implemented will restore the functioning of the principles.

Concentrated Corporate Ownership. Both Belloc and G.K. Chesterton declared that workers must become owners of the corporations that employ them. They expressed a preference for smaller, family-owned farms and businesses, but admitted that it was a preference only, not a mandate.[11]

In common with Morrison and virtually all politicians and mainstream economists, Belloc and Chesterton assumed that the only way workers or anyone else could legitimately acquire capital ownership is to cut their consumption and accumulate money savings. Even when he acknowledged that capital acquisition could be financed with borrowed money, Belloc assumed that personal savings are still required to cover consumption needs while the new capital is formed and put into production.

Requiring workers to save before they can purchase shares in the company that employs them is unnecessary, as Kelso pointed out. It is only necessary that the workers obtain credit to purchase the shares, and that the company produce and distribute profits sufficient to repay the acquisition loan. This is the basic theory of the Employee Stock Ownership Plan (ESOP) that Kelso invented.

---

[9] To paraphrase Marx and Engels in *The Communist Manifesto* very broadly.
[10] Again to paraphrase.
[11] G.K. Chesterton, *The Outline of Sanity.* Collected Works, Volume V, San Francisco, California: Ignatius Press, 1987, 148.

Money and Credit. Belloc missed the importance of the financial system in determining patterns of capital ownership. Consistent with a past savings orientation, he regarded the modern system of finance as a result, not a cause of concentrated capital ownership. As he said,

> Credit is not a vital element in all societies, it is not a permanent and general social, economic or political problem. The modern function of credit is of comparatively recent development; it has already gone woefully wrong and appears to be approaching catastrophe. Credit, then, is only a local and ephemeral issue. Nevertheless it must be dealt with, because for the moment it monstrously overshadows our civic life.[12]

Consequently, Belloc's recommendations regarding money and credit were directed to minimizing its importance and removing its influence from society as far as possible.

Taxation. As the popes noted and Belloc agreed, a high level of taxation acts both to destroy existing ownership and inhibit or prevent a program of expanded capital ownership from being successful. Kelso proposed making dividends paid by corporations tax-deductible, and then treated as ordinary taxable income by recipients. If dividends were used to make payments on a capital acquisition loan, however, any taxes would be deferred until the capital was sold, *i.e.*, total sale proceeds would be considered taxable income unless used to acquire other capital.

CESJ would also simplify personal taxation by abolishing all personal taxes except for a single-rate income tax. This single rate would be adjusted annually to meet current government expenses and reduce and finally eliminate existing debt. The tax would be imposed on all personal income from all sources above a level sufficient for a family to meet its basic needs, including shelter, healthcare, and education. By setting the income exemption at a realistic level sufficient to meet basic needs adequately, the *effective* tax rate would be zero or a small percentage at lower levels of income, and a larger percentage at higher income levels.

For example, given a single tax rate of 40%, a non-dependent exemption of $30,000, and a dependent exemption of $20,000, a family of four would pay no taxes on the first $100,000 of income, assuming that family income is aggregated for tax purposes. The effective tax rate on $200,000 of aggregate family income would be 20% or $20,000, while on $1 million would be 36% or $360,000.

---

[12] Belloc, *The Restoration of Property, op. cit.*, 141.

By making dividends tax-deductible at the corporate level, corporations would be encouraged to pay out all earnings, thereby avoiding all corporate income taxes, and restoring owners' traditional right to the full stream of income from what they own.[13] Dividends would be treated as ordinary income by the recipient, unless used to purchase a pre-determined amount of qualified capital assets, usually in the form of newly issued shares representing new growth. By permitting people to defer taxes on any income used to purchase capital assets up to the statutory limit, people could accumulate a capital stake using pre-tax income.[14]

Retail Distribution. Belloc assumed that small owners would mean small enterprises, which would be at a disadvantage when marketing to the consumer. The Just Third Way solution is the same as that for large-scale production: small owners participating in large-scale distribution on the same terms as large owners.

Sustainability of Initial Efforts. Belloc was rightfully concerned that, in the (to him) unlikely event capital ownership once again became widespread, large enterprises would take unfair advantage of smaller ones and drive them out of business. To protect small ownership, especially in its infancy, Belloc proposed the formation of legally established and protected guilds, similar to those of the Middle Ages.

Here again Belloc was blinded to some extent by his insistence that "small ownership" (widespread capital ownership) necessarily means many owners of small enterprises as sole proprietorships instead of many owners of large enterprises as joint stock companies. CESJ's solution is essentially the same as Belloc's, but with some improvements.

Instead of artificially protecting small owners by giving them favorable legal treatment such as government subsidies or putting restrictions on large enterprises, the market should determine the optimal size of enterprises. Unfair competition and monopolies should obviously be prevented or punished legally, but there should not be punitive measures taken against enterprises whether large or small when there has been no wrongdoing.

---

[13] This has been eroded due to the widespread belief that past savings are essential to finance new capital formation, thus requiring earnings to be retained instead of being paid out to the owners. See *Dodge v. Ford Motor Company*, 204 Mich. 459, 170 N.W. 668. (Mich. 1919).

[14] The full proceeds of any sale of assets on which taxes were deferred would be treated as ordinary income.

As for the interests of small owners (as distinct from small enterprises), Belloc was absolutely correct. Some sort of organization should be formed to protect the interests of small owners against large owners and to ensure that they enjoy the full rights of private property.

What to call these organizations is, of course, a matter of preference, but CESJ proposes what it calls "Ownership Unions." Ownership unions would go beyond the wage system's limitations and conflict orientation of traditional labor and craft unions.

Similar in concept to the Medieval guilds (which were associations of owners), ownership unions would serve a much broader constituency — today's non-owners as well as minority shareholders — by assisting them to organize and transform themselves into worker- and citizen-owners, and then secure and protect their ownership rights.

The Money Question

Kelso's understanding of the importance of money and credit was radically different from that of Belloc. This can be traced to Kelso's deeper understanding of an institution fundamental to the functioning of every form of economy that can possibly be conceived.

Belloc's error can be traced to the fact that, whether or not he realized it, he accepted without question a flawed theory of money. This theory, known as "the Currency Principle," not only undermines private property at the most fundamental level, it contradicts the nature of money itself.

Briefly, the Currency Principle is the theory that the amount of money and credit determine the level of economic activity in an economy. It is based on the assumption that money is a commodity, rather than (among other things) a means of measuring the value of labor and capital inputs to production, commodities, and all else of economic value.[15]

One consequence of treating money as a commodity is that it becomes subject to speculation. This drives the price of units of currency up or down, distorting the market price of actual goods and services.

---

[15] Based on the "State Theory of Money" advanced by the socialist Georg Friedrich Knapp (1842-1926), Keynes declared that currency issued by the government and backed with the government's own debt is the only legitimate money, Keynes, *A Treatise on Money, loc. cit.* Even under the Currency Principle, however, money need not be government-issued. The fallacy of the Currency Principle is the belief that production derives from money, rather than that money derives from production.

Today, all mainstream schools of economics and most of the minor ones take the Currency Principle for granted.

In contrast, binary economics is based on a theory of money and credit known as "the Banking Principle." This is the theory that the level of economic activity determines the amount of money and credit in the economy.

In its purest sense, following the Banking Principle, money is the medium of exchange. This necessarily implies that money is also a measure of value. It is impossible for two or more people to engage in a just transaction without agreeing on the equality of what is exchanged, and to do that they must have a common unit of measure. Thus, as Kelso explained,

> Money is not a part of the visible sector of the economy. People do not consume money. Money is not a physical factor of production, but rather a yardstick for measuring economic input, economic outtake and the relative values of the real goods and services of the economic world. Money provides a method of measuring obligations, rights, powers and privileges. It provides a means whereby certain individuals can accumulate claims against others, or against the economy as a whole, or against many economies. It is a system of symbols that many economists substitute for the visible sector and its productive enterprises, goods and services, thereby losing sight of the fact that a monetary system is a part only of the invisible sector of the economy, and that its adequacy can only be measured by its effect upon the visible sector.[16]

There are serious problems associated with departing from the Banking Principle and construing money and credit as a commodity. For example, if there is a standard for the currency and the standard is a commodity in limited supply, prices of all other goods and services will rise and fall in response to changes in the price of the standard, for reasons having nothing to do with the supply of and demand for the actual goods and services being exchanged. If the government controls the money supply, implements a flexible standard, and backs the currency with its own debt, the situation is much worse.

Determination of a monetary standard and proper management of a currency is a highly technical matter that we do not need to go into any further for the purposes of this discussion.[17] What is essential

---

[16] Louis O. Kelso and Patricia Hetter, *Two-Factor Theory: The Economics of Reality*. New York: Random House, 1967, 54-55.

[17] For a more in-depth treatment of monetary theory from the Just Third Way perspective, see Norman G. Kurland, "A New Look at Prices and Money: The Kelsonian

here is coming to a better understanding of what money is, by looking at what money does — or is supposed to do if the financial system adhered to the principles of the Just Third Way.

The obvious place to start is with the first principle of economics of Adam Smith (1723-1790). As Smith expressed it in *The Wealth of Nations*, "Consumption is the sole end and purpose of all production."[18] In other words, in a rational market system, nothing is produced that is not intended to be consumed by someone.

This brings us to "Say's Law of Markets." Jean-Baptiste Say did not develop the law that bears his name, but derived it from the work of Smith,[19] as Say acknowledged.[20] Say did, however, explain it better than anyone else.

Say began with Smith's first principle of economics, as he noted in his responses to Thomas Malthus. As Say argued, absent charity, theft, or some other form of redistribution, there is only one way to consume, and that is to produce.

You must either produce for your own consumption, or to have something to trade with others for what they produce that you want to consume. When governments issue money backed with their own debt, they are consuming without producing, which violates private property. Thus, as Say concluded,

> [I]n reality we do not buy articles of consumption with money, the circulating medium with which we pay for them. We must in the first instance have bought this money itself by the sale of our produce. . . . It is therefore really and absolutely with their produce that they make their purchases: therefore it is impossible for them to purchase any articles whatever, to a greater amount than those they have produced, either by themselves or through the means of their capital or their land.[21]

The best, indeed, the only legitimate way to create money, then, is to convert "produce" (*i.e.,* production) into money. Again, the details

---

Binary Model for Achieving Rapid Growth Without Inflation," *The Journal of Socio-Economics*, 30 (2001) 495-515.

[18] Adam Smith, *An Enquiry into the Nature and Causes of the Wealth of Nations*, IV.8.49.

[19] Joseph A. Schumpeter, *History of Economic Analysis, op. cit.*, 616-618. Note, however, that Schumpeter's analysis of Say's Law was taken from Say's *Treatise on Political Economy*, not Say's *Letters to Malthus*. Schumpeter also appeared to assume that Say was Currency School, which tends to confuse Schumpeter's understanding of Say's explanation of his "law."

[20] Jean-Baptiste Say, *Letters to Malthus*. London: Sherwood, Neely, and Jones, 1821, 2.

[21] *Ibid.*

of how this can be done are complex and highly technical, and they are not essential to understanding the basic theory.[22]

What we are interested in is Kelso's theoretical point. That is, money is correctly viewed as a means of engaging in, measuring, and facilitating economic transactions.

As such, in a justly structured system the amount of money and credit should be linked by private property directly to existing and future marketable goods and services. This, as John Paul II noted, would "ensur[e], by means of a stable currency and the harmony of social relations, the conditions for steady and healthy economic growth in which people through their own work can build a better future for themselves and their families.[23]

It is therefore possible to finance new capital formation by increasing production in the future instead of relying on decreasing consumption in the past. By collateralizing loans with capital credit insurance instead of with existing wealth owned by the borrower, it is possible to create sound money as needed to enable people who do not presently own capital to become capital owners.

This capital could be existing assets, but the bulk of it would probably be newly issued shares representing newly formed productive assets. It is only necessary that the new capital produce enough to pay for itself out of its own future earnings, and thereafter provide consumption income for the new owner.

Commercial and central banks were invented to expedite this process. Most modern central banks (like the U.S. Federal Reserve System) could finance a program of expanded capital ownership without requiring any new legislation. Operated properly, and all else being equal, there would always be exactly enough money and credit in the system, no more, no less, with neither inflation nor deflation.

Kelso's breakthrough in economics and finance is as profound a breakthrough as that of Pius XI in moral philosophy and social doctrine. By solving the problem of how expanded capital ownership can be financed without redistribution or restricting current

---

[22] The process of money creation for expanded capital ownership is covered in Moulton, *The Formation of Capital, op. cit.*, and Kelso and Adler, *The New Capitalists, op. cit.*

[23] *Centesimus Annus*, § 19. A stable currency requires a standard of value, which most modern currencies (even the U.S. dollar) lack. In this regard, a monetary standard based on the price of a kilowatt-hour, proposed by R. Buckminster Fuller and others, would overcome the limitations of a precious metal standard, and merits discussion.

consumption, and guided by these principles, Kelso turned Catholic social teaching from an idealistic dream into a practical reality.

As noted briefly above, however, equally significant is Kelso and Adler's presentation of economic justice as a complete system with input, out-take, and feedback-corrective principles. By defining the principle of participative justice, they offered a logical counterpart to the classical concept of distributive justice.

Their third principle of limitation, meant to discourage greed and prevent monopolies, was easily expanded into a feedback-corrective principle of "social justice," as defined by Pius XI. These three principles of participative justice, distributive justice, and social justice make the moral basis of economic personalism explicit and link the moral absolutes of Catholic social teaching directly to the realities of everyday economic life.

In combination, the principles of economic justice, binary economics, and the act of social justice have the potential to guide people in establishing and maintaining a true personalist social order that empowers and thereby respects the dignity and sovereignty of every child, woman, and man on Earth.[24]

---

[24] Kelso's invention of the Employee Stock Ownership Plan (ESOP) based on the principles of economic justice demonstrate the feasibility of universal capital ownership, even though the ESOP applies only to workers in private-sector corporations and most ESOPs do not reflect the full potential of the Just Third Way.

8
Three Principles of Economic Justice

Louis Kelso's and Mortimer Adler's breakthroughs in moral philosophy (with the principles of economic justice) and in economics and finance (with future savings) were "the missing links" in Catholic social teaching. Combined with Pius XI's definition of social justice, Kelso's and Adler's financial systems concept and principles of economic justice — connecting economic personalism with economic justice — made a truly personalist social order possible as explicit policy for the first time in history.

This was a Just Third Way that addressed the moral and structural flaws of collectivist socialism and individualist capitalism. People without capital or savings could now become capital owners without redefining private property, committing injustices against existing owners, or harming the common good.

Understanding how Kelso's and Adler's breakthroughs fit into the Just Third Way, however, requires a more detailed analysis of social justice — both as a particular and overarching social virtue and then how it is applied as a principle within a system of economic justice.

Social Justice as a Particular Virtue

In this section we will examine social justice as the overarching virtue under which economic justice must function.

As a particular virtue aimed at the perfecting of the common good, social justice has certain definable characteristics as well as basic requirements or "laws" regarding how the act of social justice is to be carried out. In his analysis of the social doctrine of Pius XI, Father William Ferree discerned seven specific laws of social justice, but added that there are probably many more. As he presented them in his pamphlet, *Introduction to Social Justice*, they are:

1. That the Common Good Be Kept Inviolate. However great our desire or need, we may not usurp the institutions of the common good to serve our private ends, no matter how important they may be to us or to others. We cannot, for example, legitimately redefine a natural right or ordinarily violate even an unjust law on our own initiative, unless the law forces us personally to do wrong. Deciding for ourselves what laws to obey is pure individualism, and is tantamount to anarchy.

It is not that we *may* not exercise private rights until the common good is corrected. Rather, it is that exercising individual rights when the common good is flawed or under attack is often *impossible*.

This is because the common good provides the environment within which individual persons become virtuous by exercising rights. When that environment is flawed, it must be materially restructured to the point where the exercise of individual rights once again becomes possible. A just system, for example, would discourage greed and prevent monopolies.

2. Cooperation, Not Conflict. Given the uniqueness of each human person, the particular good of each individual is different. Any particular good that is falsely made into an ultimate principle and exercised without any limits whatsoever must necessarily be in conflict with every other particular good.

To take an economic example, a truly free market recognizes that there are necessary limits to the exercise of rights within it, such as private property and freedom of association. To be just, a free market is not *laissez-faire*, "anything goes," but implies an effective juridical order[1] that clearly defines the exercise of individual rights, provides a level playing field, and enforces contracts when necessary. A just system would encourage virtue and discourage vice; no one is free to use his rights to harm or limit the rights of others.

Only through cooperation — people organizing for the common good — can society be structured and restructured for the good of every member. This does not mean overriding or ignoring individual goods, but it does mean that individual and social goods should not be in conflict.

3. One's First Particular Good is One's Own Place in the Common Good. The first particular good of every individual or group is how that individual or group is able to access through the institutions of the common good the means to fulfill one's human needs, acquire greater virtue or fulfill a social purpose.

This also means that each person and organization directly relates to and is responsible for the care and perfecting of a particular aspect or level of the common good. As Ferree put it,

> It must be admitted that this is not the way most of us think at the present time, but that is because we have been badly educated. It must be admitted also that to carry out such a principle in practice looks

---

[1] *Centesimus Annus*, § 42.

like too big a job for human nature as we know it; but that is because we are individualists and have missed the point. Of course it is too big a job if each one of us and each of our groups is individually and separately responsible for the welfare of the human race as a whole. But the point is that the human race as a whole is *social.*[2]

Each of us, as members of families, communities, organizations, religions, nations — *i.e.,* groups — relates to the common good in many ways and at many levels. Through our groups and institutions we interact with others, at some levels more directly or at a higher level of expertise and authority than others.

Put another way, each of us as human persons is entitled to equal access to the entirety of the common good, that vast network of laws and social institutions within which we realize our individual goods. In practical terms, then, we derive our particular or individual goods most directly through our immediate points of interaction within the common good.

4. Each Directly Responsible. Pius XI noted in § 53 of *Divini Redemptoris* that the individual is frequently helpless when confronted with socially unjust situations. That being the case, putting personal responsibility for the whole of the common good on each and every individual would appear to be an unconscionable burden.

We realize, however, that in accordance with humanity's political nature, we are not in this alone. When confronted with a situation that is impossible for the individual, the solution is first to organize at that level of the common good, even all the way up to the whole of the common good itself, if that is what is required to bring the proper forces to bear on the problem.

5. Higher Institutions Must Never Displace Lower Ones. As Ferree explained, "Another law of Social Justice which stems from the institutional character of the Common Good is that no institution in the vast hierarchy which we have seen can take over the particular actions of an institution or person below it."[3] This is the principle of "subsidiarity." For example, the principle of subsidiarity is violated when the government sets wage and price controls instead of allowing the market to function within the parameters established by individual and social justice.

It is not a question of the lower order(s) always being right, or the State taking over when the individual or group proves to be helpless

---

[2] More accurately, *political.* Ferree, *Introduction to Social Justice, op. cit.,* 36.
[3] *Ibid.,* 37.

in the face of an unjust situation. Rather, it is a case of action being carried out by individuals and groups at the most appropriate level of the common good. This is the individual or group that is "closest" to the problem, that which "subsides" within the milieu or institution, hence "subsidiarity."

6. Freedom of Association. "If every natural group of individuals has a right to its own common good and a duty towards the next highest common good, it is evident that such a group has the right to organize itself formally in view of the common good."[4] This "liberty" or "freedom of association" is a natural right, so important as to be ranked with the triad of life, liberty, and private property as the means whereby each individual can pursue happiness, that is, become virtuous, fulfilling the purpose for which the social order exists.

Freedom of association has frequently been interpreted in economic and social justice as limited to the right of labor to organize and demand higher fixed wages and more benefits. This increases costs and raises prices to customers, harming the poor and restricting global trade.[5]

Consequently, workers usually fail to organize for ownership, the recommended solution to many of the social problems they attempt to address by raising wages and benefits.[6] Others assume that it refers to organizing for civil rights, which soon become meaningless without the economic rights to sustain them.

7. All Vital Interests Should be Organized. All real and vital interests of life should be deliberately made to conform to the requirements of the common good. As Ferree noted, social justice "is a full-time job that never ends."[7]

This can make the task seem overwhelming until we realize that, as social justice is the virtue directed at the common good, the bulk of the work is done once we as individuals have internalized the basic precepts of the natural law that underpin the social order, summarized as "good is to be done, evil avoided."

---

[4] *Ibid.*, 38.
[5] Walter Reuther (1907-1970), president of the United Auto Workers union, advocated that workers receive increases from profits instead of higher wages, thereby raising consumption income without increasing costs. As he said, "Since profits are a residual, after all costs have been met, and since their size is not determinable until after customers have paid the prices charged for the firm's products, profit sharing as such cannot be said to have any inflationary impact upon costs and prices." (Testimony before the Joint Economic Committee of Congress, February 20, 1967.)
[6] *Rerum Novarum*, §§ 46-47.
[7] Ferree, *Introduction to Social Justice, op. cit.*, 40.

After that, it is not a question of adding more tasks to an already overloaded life, but of doing the same things in a different way — more effectively, as we might expect, and certainly in a manner more consistent with our own nature, but still the same basic tasks directed at becoming virtuous, or maintaining us in that endeavor.

The Characteristics of Social Justice

In addition to the laws of social justice, social justice has certain characteristics. These are,

1. Only By Members of Groups. The principal characteristic of social justice is possibly the most difficult concept to grasp. That is, social justice cannot be performed by individuals *as individuals*, but only by individuals *as members of groups*.

Addressing flawed institutions under social justice does not mean making up for the failure of individual justice or charity. The proper course of action is to organize with others, then, as members of groups, work on correcting the institutions so that they function so as to allow individual virtues to function once again.[8]

2. It Takes Time. All virtue is the habit of doing good, and habits, especially social habits, take time to build, just as vice (the habit of doing evil), individual or social, is not something that happens overnight. In social justice, time must be taken to educate, persuade others, and organize with others to "fix the system."

3. Nothing is Impossible. In social justice there is never any such thing as helplessness. As Ferree stated, "No problem is ever too big or too complex, no field is ever too vast, for the methods of this social justice. Problems that were agonizing in the past and were simply dodged, even by serious and virtuous people, can now be solved with ease by any school child."[9]

4. Eternal Vigilance. The work of social justice is never finished. This is not the same as saying that social justice takes a long time. Rather, it means we must be constantly prepared to respond to what Pius XI called "the radical instability of society." Different people come into the picture, conditions change, technology advances, and our institutions must be restructured and reformed to meet the new conditions. This change is always happening; therefore the work of social justice is continual.[10]

---

8 Kelso and Adler, *The Capitalist Manifesto, op. cit.*, 161.
9 Ferree, *Introduction to Social Justice, op. cit.*, 47.
10 *Ibid.*, 49-50.

5. Effectiveness. Work for the common good must be effective. You cannot just do something and simply hope it works. A good intention to benefit the common good is not good enough. We may gratify ourselves with a feeling of great virtue, but we have not fulfilled our responsibilities under social justice until we have organized and acted with others to correct a particular defect in the common good.

6. You Cannot "Take It or Leave It." As Ferree stated, social justice embraces a "rigid obligation." Each of us is directly and individually responsible for our level or area of the common good, and we must organize with others to bring about necessary institutional reform.

Social justice is not, however, something we add to the tasks of everyday life. Rather, it is a fundamental change in *how* we do what we do as political animals — acting in an organized, social manner with others, rather than ineffectually as isolated individuals.

The Framework of Economic Justice

As we discussed in Chapter 2, social justice is the particular virtue directed to the common good, and is therefore the class of justice within which economic justice — the particular virtue directed to the economic common good — functions. Economic justice is thus the application of social justice to a particular part of the common good, *viz.*, the economy.

Perhaps confusing matters, social justice also operates as one of the three principles of economic justice. Social justice serves as the balancing and corrective principle of a universally participative and just market economy.

To explain, in common with Taparelli and his principle of social justice, Kelso and Adler presented their breakthrough as principles (guiding concepts or rules) and not particular virtues (which require an action directed at a particular object). This is understandable, given Adler's classical orientation toward the individual virtues, and takes nothing away from the fact that they gave substance and structure to the term "economic justice."

This was a profound breakthrough in moral philosophy in and of itself. CESJ later refined Kelso and Adler's principles by identifying them as particular virtues within the framework of social virtue as presented in the social doctrine of Pius XI and analyzed by Father William Ferree. As noted briefly in the previous chapter, then, the principles of economic justice are,

- **Participative Justice,** or the input principle,
- **Distributive Justice,** or the out-take principle, and
- **Social Justice,** or the feedback and corrective principle.

Before going further, a caveat is in order. The principles of economic justice must be understood as components of a coherent system. No part or principle can be taken in isolation or exaggerated without regard to the others.

Like the legs of a tripod, if even one is missing or flawed, the whole structure collapses. Taken together, the three principles of economic justice provide the framework for the most just and stable forms of the economic order.

The Input Principle: Participative Justice

Participative justice is the particular virtue relating to the natural equality of every human being as a human being. In terms of economic justice, participative justice involves the production side of an economy. That is, how each person and family contributes to the production of wealth, thus earning a proportionate (just) share of the wealth that is distributed (*i.e.,* distributive justice).[11]

Kelso and Adler appear to have been the first to introduce a specific concept of participative justice, defining it as:

> [The requirement] to organize the economy in such a way that every man or family can use his or its property [in both labor and capital] to participate in the production of wealth in a way that earns a living for that man or family.[12]

They point out that the right of every person to produce the wealth he needs, relates to all other natural rights, starting with the right to life. The right to participate in economic production,

> . . . derives immediately from the most fundamental among all of man's natural rights — his right to life or existence. The right to life involves more than a right not to be murdered or maimed. Since a man cannot live for long without having the means of subsistence, the right to life is meaningless unless it involves a right to acquire subsistence by rightful means.[13]

The right to earn a subsistence through participation in the production of wealth, Kelso and Adler explain, can be violated in several

---

[11] Kelso and Adler, Chapter 5, Economic Justice and Economic Rights, *The Capitalist Manifesto,* 78.
[12] *Ibid.,* 78.
[13] *Ibid.,* 78.

ways: 1) denial of one's life, liberty and property (the right of control over one's labor and capital, and the right to the full fruits of what one produces through one's labor or capital), or 2) where one's property in labor or capital is rendered ineffective under prevailing economic conditions as a means for earning a living (such as occurred when the invention of automobiles eliminated the demand for buggy whips).

This leads to their critical insight that having property only in one's labor, may become insufficient for earning a decent living, particularly as technology renders certain forms of labor obsolete:

> Hence in an industrial economy, and especially in one that is technologically advanced, the right to obtain subsistence by earning it involves more than the right to work and the right to a just return for work done. It involves the right to participate effectively in the production of wealth by means consistent with the existing state of technology and with the greatest technological advances of which the economy is capable.[14]

Participative justice does not guarantee equal or predetermined results. It does, however, require that society's institutions (or those charged with the care of those institutions) guarantee every person the equal human right to make a productive contribution to the economy, both through one's labor (as a worker) and through one's productive capital (as an owner). Participative justice provides equal opportunity to every person to participate with his labor or capital as needed to produce goods and services in a free market system.

Thus, this equal opportunity-based principle of participation — participative justice — rejects monopolies, special privileges, and other exclusionary social barriers that inhibit or prevent economic self-reliance (the means to sustain life) and personal freedom (liberty).

The Out-take Principle: Distributive Justice

Distributive justice, in one sense, is an individual virtue built on commutative justice, commutative justice being the most basic form of justice. As an individual virtue, distributive justice relates to how incomes are distributed to individual producers in a market economy. Operating as a social virtue in a free market economy, distributive justice guides economic institutions with respect to the income distribution or consumption side of the economic equation.

---

[14] Kelso and Adler, *The Capitalist Manifesto*, 80.

Commutative justice — strict justice — is the justice of contracts, of exchange, and exchange presumes equality. Equality being the essence of justice, all forms of justice ultimately derive from commutative justice and cannot violate, dismiss, or ignore it. In common with all forms of justice, distributive justice assumes the validity of commutative justice, or it could not be considered a true natural right.

We discussed the justice-based (as opposed to charity-based) principle of distribution — distributive justice — at some length in Chapter 2. It is therefore only necessary to give a brief recap here, noting, however, that the equality that characterizes distributive justice is distribution (out-take) based on each one's proportionate contribution (inputs).

As applied in economic justice, then, distributive justice is the out-take principle described in legal terms as the form of justice "which should govern the distribution of rewards and punishments. It assigns to each person the rewards which his or her personal merit or services deserve, or the proper punishment for his crimes."[15] Distributive justice reflects the equal right of each person to receive his full and proper due in proportion to the inputs of, and what is due to, others.

The classical form of distributive justice found in the Magisterium of the Catholic Church[16] as well as in the Just Third Way is based on the exchange or market value of one's economic contributions. This is the principle that all people have an equal right to receive a proportionate, share of the value of the marketable goods and services they produce with others, through their labor contributions, their capital contributions, or both. As Kelso and Adler explain,

> Considering *only* those who are engaged in the production of wealth, and relying on free and workable competition as the only way to ascertain the facts about the equal or unequal value of the contributions made by each of a number of independent participants in production, distributive justice is done if the share (whether in the form of wages, dividends, rents, etc.) received by each participant in production is proportionate to the value of his contribution to production.[17]

Distributive justice must be extended equally to all participants in the productive process regardless of their social status, condition, or characteristic. It can only operate under conditions of a truly free and

---

[15] "Justice," *Black's Law Dictionary*. St. Paul, Minnesota: West Publishing Company, 1951.
[16] *Compendium of the Social Doctrine of the Church*, § 201.
[17] Kelso and Adler, *The Capitalist Manifesto, op. cit.,* 70.

non-monopolistic marketplace that respects every participant's full rights of private property.

This is because in a free market, unlike a command or State-controlled economy, every person as a producer or consumer votes with his money, determining for himself what something being exchanged is worth, rather than having a bureaucrat, technocrat, or wise man make that judgment for that individual.

Given the increasing use of labor-eliminating technology within a modern economy, producers who have only their labor to contribute to production have found that under distributive justice, they are due a resulting share of the wealth produced (or income thereof) that is insufficient for supporting themselves and their families. Without access to capital ownership, non-owning workers must turn more to coercive measures through the State or labor unions to receive livable incomes.

The Feedback and Corrective Principle: Social Justice

As a principle of economic justice, social justice governs how participative justice and distributive justice function with regard to the good of individual persons, but also looks to the structuring of economic institutions and the common good as a whole. When the principle of social justice is added to the principles of participative and distributive justice, economic justice becomes something specifically social.

Social justice is thus the feedback principle that detects violations of participative and distributive justice in a system or institution. It rebalances (or enables) participative justice and distributive justice to function again when the system deviates materially from either essential principle.

Social justice includes a concept of limitation that discourages greed and monopolies, which prevent most people from equal opportunity and access to the means to participate fully in the economy as capital owners.[18] Frequently problems with wealth and income distribution can be traced to a problem with, or lack of, participative justice in the institution or system itself.

---

[18] Kelso and Adler originally called this third principle of economic justice the principle of limitation, and specifically mentioned greed and monopolies as targets for limitation. As this was inadequate in light of the social doctrine of Pius XI and the personalism of John Paul II, CESJ expanded it to the more comprehensive term social justice. Kelso and Adler, *The Capitalist Manifesto, op. cit.*, 68, 82-86.

Enabling every person to enjoy the universal human right to become an owner of productive capital becomes increasingly critical with respect to the act of social justice itself — organizing with others to build and maintain a just social, political and economic order. Capital ownership enables people to more fully carry out their social duty to the common good, in fact, when they are able to participate in it as capital owners, empowered, independent, and responsible. As Father William Ferree noted,

> Man is a social being and is bound to aid and support the Common Good of himself and his fellows. He can best discharge this obligation when he is owner of the things he administers and is thus free to direct them to the Common Good in his use. An agency responsibility is always narrower than the responsibility of ownership; so a full preoccupation for the Common Good can exist only in one who has the broad responsibility of ownership.[19]

[19] Rev. William J. Ferree, S.M., Ph.D., "A Turning Point in History," *Every Worker an Owner*. Arlington, Virginia: Center for Economic and Social Justice, 1987, 32.

9
Four Policy Pillars

Combining Louis Kelso's innovation in economics and finance, and with Mortimer Adler the clearly defined principles of economic justice, along with Pius XI's revolution in social philosophy lays the groundwork for economic personalism. In this way, economic institutions — including the policies and laws governing those institutions — can be structured in a way the respects the dignity of every person. The result is a *Just* Third Way that transcends the flaws inherent in collectivism that manifests as socialism, and individualism that finds expression in capitalism.

Like any theory, however, economic personalism requires clear guidelines in order to apply principles in a practical way to achieve a more just and humane future for all. Sound theory is essential, but to be effective it must be put into practice without violating its own principles. The end does not justify the means.

Reconnecting Persons to Society

With respect to the demands of economic and social justice, the primary task is to integrate the exercise of each person's inalienable natural rights (especially life, liberty, and private property) into the institutional structure of the common good. This must be done so as to optimize the exercise of individual rights to the advantage of the whole of society, or at the very least do no harm.

As originally conceived, this was the idea of the system implemented by the U.S. Constitution. It was the reason the American political system has been commended by almost every pope since Pius IX. Orestes Augustus Brownson (1803-1876) put it well in the Introduction to *The American Republic* (1866),

> The United States, or the American Republic, has a mission, and is chosen of God for the realization of a great idea. . . . its mission is not so much the realization of liberty as the realization of the true idea of the State, which secures at once the authority of the public and the freedom of the individual — the sovereignty of the people without social despotism, and individual freedom without anarchy.[1]

---

[1] Orestes A. Brownson, *The American Republic: Its Constitution, Tendencies and Destiny.* Wilmington, Delaware: ISI Books, 2003, 3.

Sometimes, however, the institutional structure within which individuals exercise their rights becomes distorted or flawed. Usually this involves the law, but it also includes custom, tradition, and any other social structure that guides individual behavior within groups, and of smaller groups within larger groups.

When the institutional environment becomes flawed, each individual in that society has the personal responsibility to organize with others to effect changes in the surrounding institutions. As the goal of the act of social justice, this ensures that every person has equal access to the common good, including the means to secure one's own dignity, empowerment, and development.

As was seen in the Papal States under Pius IX, this presents a problem if people are not well-grounded in the principles of personalism, or if they are not prepared to apply those principles in a practical way. Constitutional scholar Albert Venn Dicey (1835-1922), for example, noted that no law is likely to have the desired effect unless people are prepared to accept the law and obey it in the manner intended. Nor can the State force compliance. It must come from people themselves.[2]

---

[2] See Albert Venn Dicey, *Lectures on the Relation Between Law and Public Opinion in England During the Nineteenth Century.* New Brunswick, New Jersey: Transaction Books, 1981.

People must therefore come together in social charity,[3] loving their institutions as they love themselves and their neighbors. As Father William Ferree explained, instead of destroying them, we must understand our institutions and identify their flaws (often artificial barriers to equal opportunity and access to the means to participate fully) in order to determine what corrections we need to make in those systems and institutions. By organizing with others to correct the system, our institutions can then once again be in material conformity with the natural law and the principles of personalism.

Only in the spirit of social charity and its process of understanding our institutions and their social purposes can people organize effectively. They can then carry out acts of social justice with the directed intent of bringing about the necessary changes in the institutional environment.

The State's role, then, is not to try and coerce desired results or command them by fiat. Rather, the State should assist organized groups to make the required and appropriate changes in their institutions and laws, and enforce them when necessary.

Moving from the personalist theory of social restructuring in general, we are now prepared to look at the personalist application of social restructuring of the economic order in particular. That is, we must reconcile the common good at the level of the economy with the economic good of each person, and we must do so without harming or unnecessarily limiting either.

In personalism we must always keep in mind that the purpose of society is to assist individuals in becoming virtuous. The first guideline to keep in mind, therefore, is that the State is made for man, not man for the State. The State, frankly, is only a social tool presumably designed by and created to assist people, not the other way around.

Second, we must also keep in mind that no coerced act is truly virtuous. A State that mandates how people are required to live is fundamentally different from one in which people are free to act as they see fit within established parameters. A personalist social order is one that respects freedom of choice as far as possible, without violating the lives and rights of others.

Third, a personalist society requires that all persons have power. A person is that which has rights, and it is generally only by the exercise of rights that persons become virtuous. Persons that do not have

---

[3] *Caritas in Veritate,* § 78.

the power to exercise rights are inhibited from becoming virtuous, as they become the objects or tools of others.

Fourth and finally, persons without power must have the means of obtaining power, and those with power must have the means of securing it. We can therefore gauge whether or not a society is just and truly personalist not merely by observing whether everyone has the equal opportunity and means to gain power, but also how power is obtained and maintained.

Applying these general guidelines to economic life, we distill them into four tenets that aim to secure both the possession and the optimal exercise of our natural rights within the common good of the economy. We can therefore call these the "Four Policy Pillars of a Just Market Economy":

- **Widespread direct capital ownership,** individually or in free association with others (the "fatal omission" from the major schools of economics today),
- **A limited economic role for the State,** so that economic power resides in all the citizens and the State remains economically dependent on its citizens,
- **Free, open, and non-monopolistic markets,** within a strong juridical order as the best means of determining just wages, just prices, and just profits, and
- **Restoration of the rights of private property,** especially in corporate equity.

Similar to the way that the three principles of economic justice must be understood as integrated elements of a system if they are to be effective, the four policy pillars of a just market economy provide the fundamental guidelines for establishing laws and practical measures to create a personalist economy. We will now examine them in order:

Widespread Direct Capital Ownership

Higher wages or better benefits are not the goal of economic personalism. The hallmark of an economically just society (and, more broadly, of social justice) is its systematic approach to balancing the demands of participative and distributive justice by lifting institutional barriers which have historically denied equal ownership opportunities to every citizen. As Pius XI declared in *Divini Redemptoris,*

Society cannot defraud man of his God-granted rights. Nor can society systematically void these rights by making their use impossible. It is therefore according to the dictates of reason that ultimately all material things should be ordained to man as a person, that through his mediation they may find their way to the Creator.[4]

A major flaw in the wage system is not simply that it limits most people's income to what they can get from selling their labor, but that wages are given, granted, or gained through government intervention or collective bargaining pressures backed up with the threat of State intervention. This runs counter to the demands of an economically just society, in which persons exercise free choice within a system of equal ownership opportunities and checks-and-balances to keep power spread to every person.

Most proposals for social betterment, whether capitalist, socialist, or Welfare/Servile State, focus on increasing income or providing benefits directly. This, as the solidarist labor economist Goetz Antony Briefs (1889-1974) noted in his book, *The Proletariat* (1937), is inevitable when most people lack capital ownership. As Briefs, a student of Father Heinrich Pesch, S.J. (1854-1926), explained,

> The higher standard of living for the worker has been gained at the sacrifice of economic independence and self-reliance along many fronts, and the process still goes on. The picture has, of course, its reverse side. The workers to whom these benefits have accrued have less and less chance to improve their status. Wage earners have become established in the proletarian mode of existence, this being the price exacted by capitalism for its alleviation of their lot. Let this process be carried to its logical conclusion, and what is the result? An industrial seigniory, extended over great drab masses of economic dependents, individuals whose life depends on their finding or keeping a job. The area which used to be occupied by self-respecting, self-reliant property owners with small or medium-sized holdings — the home territory of the bourgeoisie and the breeding place of democracy — is so no more.[5]

While Pesch did not recognize a particular act of social justice, he described private property as one of the "three institutional 'pillars' of economic society."[6] The others are "marriage and the family" and "the State as guardian of the positive legal order required by the value and rights of man."[7]

When Pesch wrote, Austrian and German Catholic socialists insisted that property is merely prudential. This, obviously, was simply

---

[4] *Divini Redemptoris*, § 30.
[5] Briefs, *The Proletariat, op. cit.*, 252.
[6] Gustav Gundlach, S.J., "Solidarist Economics, Philosophy and Socio-economic Theory in Pesch" *Social Order*, April 1951, 185.
[7] *Ibid.*

a restatement of their traditional dogma that private property should be abolished. It was also, in part, a direct reaction to Pesch's unyielding stance on the sacredness of private property. As Alfred Diamant (1917-2012) explained,

> Because man was the center of the social system, he also was at the center of economic activity. Therefore, Pesch accepted the principle of wage labor and of the separation of labor and capital. (*Lehrbuch der Nationalökonomie*, 1, 17 – 18)[8] He demanded, however, that the community, acting through the State, interfere to prevent capitalist excesses which might threaten the economic status of individuals, and especially their private property which they must have to be able to fulfill their function in society. (*Ibid.*, 1, 188, 206 – 207)[9]

Commentators who consider widespread capital ownership prudential matter forget there has never been a society that, having redefined the institution of private property, avoided a similar redefinition of life and liberty. This inevitably undermined the power and therefore the dignity of the human person. By challenging the primary means intended by God to sustain human life and liberty and support the dignity of the human person in the temporal sphere, socialists effectively redefine what it means to be human, as well as what it means to be alive or free.

There is also the problem of the fundamental principle of socialism, that meeting material needs relegates everything else, especially capital ownership, to unimportance; the end justifies the means. As Hilaire Belloc said of the various schemes such as social credit, they are not concerned with property, that is, with power, but with income.[10]

Admittedly, redistribution would solve the problem of how propertyless workers are to meet their survival needs. It would, however, do nothing to assist them in becoming virtuous, which is (after all), the primary goal of Catholic social teaching, not the creation of a race of happy and satisfied slaves.

A Limited Economic Role for the State

Limiting the economic power of the State is essential to a system of economic personalism. This is especially important given the temptation to which many world leaders succumb of passing laws to force

---

[8] Body notes as in the quoted text.
[9] Alfred Diamant, *Austrian Catholics and the Social Question, 1918-1933*. Gainesville, Florida: University of Florida Press, 1959, 21.
[10] Belloc, *The Restoration of Property, op. cit.*, 9.

people to act in ways the power *élite* (whether public or private) view as desirable. Further, when the State tries to take over control of everyday life, the State becomes "overwhelmed and crushed by almost infinite tasks and duties."[11]

As a social tool, it is the nature of the State to be a monopoly. This consists of control over coercion as a means of enforcing goals which society has already accepted and internalized. Since monopolies *ipso facto* limit choice, the State should not own anything that could be owned and controlled directly and democratically by people.

In a personalist social order, God vests political sovereignty in persons who in turn delegate it to the State. Since the State is the only legitimate civil monopoly, its power must therefore be subject to checks and balances and democratic accountability.

Ultimate sovereignty of every person can be maintained only if economic power is kept directly in the hands of the people, both as an inherent right and as a safeguard and protection against their own rulers. In general, the economic power of the State should be limited to,

- Encouraging private sector growth and policing abuses,
- Ending economic monopolies and special privileges,
- Removing barriers to equal ownership opportunities,
- Protecting property, enforcing contracts, and settling disputes,
- Preventing inflation and providing a stable currency,
- Promoting democratic unions to protect worker and ownership rights,
- Protecting the environment, and
- Promoting or providing social safety nets.

Thus, as Leo XIII summed up the proper way to view the role of the State, "Man precedes the State, and possesses, prior to the formation of any State, the right of providing for the substance of his body."[12]

Free and Open Markets

In personalism, a limited economic role for the State means that everyone, rather than a private sector or State *élite*, exercises economic power. That in turn necessarily implies free and open markets. Within an understandable and fair system of laws, the free market is

---

[11] *Quadragesimo Anno*, § 78.
[12] *Rerum Novarum*, § 7.

the most objective and democratic means for determining just prices, just wages and just profits (the residual after all goods or services are sold). As Leo XIII said,

> Let the working man and the employer make free agreements, and in particular let them agree freely as to the wages; nevertheless, there underlies a dictate of natural justice more imperious and ancient than any bargain between man and man.[13]

The history of civilization demonstrates the consequences to society when the market is restricted and controlled by a few. Eventually, those who control the market for goods and services control the marketplace of ideas. Economic freedom and intellectual honesty seem to be inseparable.

A free and open market is one in which economic value judgments and choices are made by many people, not just a few. The greater the number of people who vote with their own economic power, the more objective and democratic the results.

Where only a few have the power to determine prices, wages and profits, their judgments are necessarily more subjective and arbitrary. When the State, the capitalist, or even the labor union is in a position to dictate wages, prices and profits, the result is a tyranny over the marketplace, and — eventually — control over people's subsistence.

Establishing a free, open and non-monopolistic and open market would be accomplished by implementing the following reforms:

- Gradually eliminating all special privileges and monopolies created by the State,
- Reducing all subsidies except for the neediest members of society,
- Removing barriers to free trade and free labor, and
- Ending all State-controlled or collectivist methods of determining prices, wages and profits.

Restoration of Private Property

Every person absolutely has the natural right to acquire and possess property. As a corollary, each person's absolute right to be an owner necessarily implies that an individual owner's exercise of the rights of ownership must be limited, as there would be chaos if every owner tried to exercise his rights without regard to the rights of

---

[13] *Ibid.*, § 45.

others. In general, an owner must exercise his ownership in a manner befitting the demands of human dignity and the common good as a whole.

As ownership and control have been separated in many instances throughout the world today, restoration of the rights of private property, especially in corporate equity, is an essential pillar of an economically just society. Owners' rights in private property are fundamental to any just economic order, as the popes have pointed out. Property secures personal choice, and, as John Locke observed, is the key safeguard of all other human rights.

Again, property is not the possession itself, but the natural right to be an owner, and the socially determined and limited bundle of rights and powers that owners have in their relationships to their possessions. Where society wants to de-monopolize access to ownership and profits in the nation's productive enterprises, it must also restore the original personal rights of property in the means of production. As Kelso put it, "Property in everyday life, is the right of *control*"[14] as well as enjoyment of the income.

Under socialism, the goal is to abolish private property in capital. By destroying private property, however, justice is denied. Without private property there is no means to empower the individual economically. Private property is the individual's link to the economic process in the same way that the secret ballot is his link to the political process. When either is absent, the individual is disconnected or alienated from the process — from his milieu, his natural environment.

Restoring the idea as well as the fact of private property involves the reform of laws that prohibit or inhibit acquisition and possession of private property. This would include ensuring that all owners, including shareholders, are vested with their full rights to participate in control of their productive property, to hold management accountable through shareholder representatives on the corporate board of directors, and to receive profits commensurate with their ownership stakes.

Owners' rights of private property are the economic equivalent of the ballot for creating an effective economic democracy within a

---

[14] Louis O. Kelso, "Karl Marx: The Almost Capitalist," *American Bar Association Journal*, March 1957; Belloc, *Restoration of Property, op. cit.*, 16-17. Cf. Rev. Matthew Habiger, O.S.B., Ph.D., *Papal Teachings on Private Property, 1891-1981.* Lanham, Maryland: University Press of America, 1990.

competitive free enterprise system. That is why ownership was included in Article 17 of the United Nations' Universal Declaration of Human Rights.[15]

Restoring owners' full rights in private property results in securing personal choices and economic self-determination for every citizen. It links income distribution to economic participation, not only by present owners of existing assets, but also by new owners of future wealth.

As nearly all the popes from Leo XIII to Francis have asserted, people should control what is owned and enjoy the income it generates. We must own, not be owned. "A working man's little estate . . . should be as completely at his full disposal[16] as are the wages he receives for his labor. But it is precisely in such power of disposal that ownership obtains, whether the property consist of land or chattels."[17]

This brings us back to the importance to social justice of the monetary and tax reforms for which Louis Kelso called as an integral part of his expanded capital ownership proposal. Without the financially feasible and morally just way of financing expanded capital ownership that Kelso contributed to the discussion, Catholic social teaching would always have remained just talk, and socialism would be the only recourse — and a rather hopeless one.

Once, however, we are freed from what Kelso called the "slavery of [past] savings" imposed by reliance on the flawed principles of mainstream economics, especially that of Keynes, new possibilities open up. It becomes possible to escape the trap in which the human race has ensnared itself, and work toward the establishment and maintenance of an economically (and thus politically) just society.

The process involves conforming ourselves as far as possible to the natural law based on God's Nature self-realized in His Intellect and discernible by human reason. At the same time, we must apply the precepts of the law to our institutions to make the task of conforming ourselves to the law not so much easier, per se, as the most advantageous or optimal behavior of reasonable beings striving to become virtuous within a justly structured social order.

---

[15] "Article 17: (1) Everyone has the right to own property alone as well as in association with others. (2) No one shall be arbitrarily deprived of his property."

[16] In context, "disposal" refers to control and enjoyment of the income.

[17] Rerum Novarum, § 5. A "chattel" is a non-landed piece of property or a fixture thereto.

By applying the precepts of the natural law, especially in regard to private property in capital, we have both the necessary personal orientation and the social principles to develop a personalist economic program. This would empower people economically and foster respect for the dignity and sovereignty of the human person under God.

The question then becomes which specific institutions need to be targeted for immediate reform and as the objects of acts of social justice.

10
Five Levers of Change

In social and economic justice, there is no "one size fits all." Applying the principles of economic personalism to any particular society is and will always remain more of an art than a science. The question of which institutions need to be reformed and what will be the most effective means to do this is one that cannot be resolved easily. At the same time the question must be settled before any effective action can be taken.

It is therefore essential that the general philosophy and specific principles of personalism outlined in this book be understood thoroughly before organizing for acts of social justice. That means going beyond the contents of this book, which can only scratch the surface.

Only then can it be determined if a proposed reform, regardless how feasible or expedient it appears at first glance, is consistent with the dignity of every human person, which (after all) should be our most immediate concern, particularly when applying Catholic social teaching. It must also be consistent with human nature and the meaning and purpose of life: to become virtuous. In practical terms, this means pursuing happiness, working for the common good, and serving God.

Assuming that the principles and approaches of economic personalism are consistent with human dignity and natural law, how can they help us transform the economic and social order, that is, change the overall system? In observing social movements that have brought about systemic change, we can see five major "levers of change," or institutional tools of social justice. These have proven the most pivotal for effecting institutional change in modern society:

- **Education,**
- **Politics,**
- **Money and Credit,**
- **Tax Policy, and**
- **Technology.**

Since specifics will rely on the conditions and needs of a particular culture and people, we cannot say with absolute certainty what final form these levers of change should take. We can, however, insist that, to be consistent with personalism, both means and ends must conform to natural law.

Education

Few people would disagree that Academia is seriously in need of reform. In many countries "education" at home and in school has changed not merely its purpose, but its nature. It has shifted from training people how to think and to become virtuous, to job training and human programming — "social engineering." Education nowadays prepares people for jobs that may be obsolete by the time they enter the workforce.

Academia, however, is the institution in need of reform, not the means by which it is reformed. Education is the tool, the lever, to initiate change not merely in Academia, but in the whole of society.

By "education" we mean the initial process of transmitting to each person in society a sound framework of universal principles. These are the tools with which to understand the world and new ideas, develop analytical and critical skills, and learn how to think as a free human being.

Once we have such a framework and principles, the task in social justice becomes one of teaching the teachers. This makes sense, as before we can, for example, reach out to the young, we need to realign and clarify what is taught. One cannot teach what one does not know. From the perspective of personalism, what is taught must conform to strict principles of natural law, personalism, and social justice.

It is also essential to make fundamental changes not merely in what is taught, but in how and to what end people are educated in the home, the schools, organized religion, and even the workplace. This, as we saw in Chapter 3, is the "social charity phase" of the act of social justice. It consists of understanding the institution that is in need of reform. This includes not merely learning the techniques or methods of social justice, but of the particular institution — that is, its place in the common good (its purpose) — and defining the problem in the institution that needs to be addressed.

Unlike other creatures that conform instinctively to their inherent nature, human beings must learn — be educated — in what it means to become more fully human and how to do so. That is, where all other things have an actual, determinate nature, human beings have a potential, determinable nature.[1]

---

[1] Adler, *Truth in Religion, op. cit.*, 154.

As human beings we do not automatically love others or our institutions as we love ourselves. We must be taught to give that essential gift of self that constitutes the act of social charity.

Only after we have learned the principles of personalism and how to apply them to the social order using the *techniques* or methods of social justice are we able to carry out *acts* of social justice to create "structures of virtue." By embedding this new paradigm into the fabric of society we can build an environment wherein people have the opportunity and means to become virtuous, that is, become more fully human.

Only then will it be possible to reform Academia to study seriously the premises, values, theoretical constructs, and so on, of the Just Third Way of personalism and economic personalism.

Politics

In the Aristotelian, philosophical sense, politics refers to the behavior of human beings as "political animals" having both individual and social aspects. In this broad sense, politics refers to the art of securing and maintaining fundamental human rights of all persons without harm to other individuals, groups, or the common good as a whole. Social justice is the particular virtue directed to the common good by means of which this social order is structured, reformed, and maintained.

In the narrower sense, politics refers to the relations between the human person and the State, the State being the organized group or institution having a delegated responsibility for the common good. Politics in this sense consists of those organized actions that require both servant leaders and a critical mass of educated and committed people to develop the formal political system. Generally, this is done by enacting good laws that will maintain good institutions, or reform flawed institutions.

It is when laws and institutions are unjust or flawed that the political nature of social justice and its role in establishing and maintaining the Just Third Way of Economic Personalism becomes essential. This is especially the case when leaders fail to act in correcting, or even acknowledging, defects in the system.

One of the goals of education should be the formation of a critical mass of change agents. This should start with a core of highly committed, disciplined, and articulate people who have internalized the principles of personalism and economic justice. These change agents should be organized into local groups all directed to the same general objective of the restructuring of the social order.[2]

This was Pope Pius XI's program for reformed Catholic Action. Although specifically not political in the limited, modern sense,[3] Catholic Action was intended to be quintessentially political in the much broader, Aristotelian sense. It also seems evident, given Pius XI's universal outlook, that he envisioned Catholic Action as the model for organized social action by Catholics as well as a model and prototype organization for those of other faiths and philosophies.

Well-organized groups should be formed in which the members have internalized the fundamental principles that define the group (solidarity), in order to develop and organize to implement an effective personalist program as an alternative to the disorder seen today in every sphere of life. This can have an effect far greater than the relatively small size of those groups might suggest, particularly when they focus on influencing key people in other groups, especially Academia and lawmakers.[4]

Servant leadership plays an important role in the Just Third Way. As individuals, persons are particularly or directly responsible for becoming virtuous. Organized into groups, persons *as members of groups* are particularly or directly responsible for the virtue of the institutions within which they subside. All persons, whether as individuals or members of groups, have a general or indirect responsibility for the whole of the common good.

Charged with particular or direct care of the common good, servant leaders are those individuals chosen by others to exercise authority to carry out this responsibility. Whether they lead particular institutions within the State or of the State itself, servant leaders guide the institution or State and the people in becoming virtuous within the structured environment of the common good.

---

[2] Norman G. Kurland, "How to Win a Revolution . . . And Enjoy It," CESJ occasional paper, 1989 (revised), 13.

[3] This was primarily an effort to forestall interference from Mussolini's government. Fascist Italy and Nazi Germany, although ostensibly organized to the point few other societies have achieved, permitted few institutions or activities not under the direct control of the State. This, as George Sabine noted, left the individual utterly unprotected from abusive State power. In general, and explaining why it is always the first natural right to be undermined, this degree of State power is only possible when private property has been eroded or abolished. Sabine, *A History of Political Theory, op. cit.*, 915-921.

[4] Kurland, "How to Win a Revolution," *op. cit.*, 13-14.

As guided by the spirit of personalism in the teachings of Martin Luther King, Jr., the 1960s civil rights movement in the United States provides a good example of how people without power can organize for peaceful social change to be embodied later in law. Although the movement limited its economic goals to jobs and welfare (rather than equal citizen access to money power and capital ownership opportunities), its application of peaceful "People Power" to achieve the political goal of "one person, one vote" demonstrated the strength of personalist principles and effectiveness of acts of social justice.

Money and Credit

As we have seen, the meaning and purpose of life — becoming virtuous to become more fully human — requires that people have power. As a rule, in order to have power, people must have private property. In order to have private property and be secure in its possession, people must have access to the means of acquiring and possessing private property, and that requires access to the just and responsible use of money and credit.

In Chapter 2 we covered the fundamentals of a just money and credit system. Given that, we understand that all money — particularly the currency — must be:

- **Asset-Backed,** based directly on something with a tangible, measurable value sufficient to meet the requirements of consideration in a valid contract (this precludes a government issuing currency backed with its own debt),

- **Elastic,** expand and contract directly with the needs of the economy,

- **Stable,** not subject to fluctuations in value, and

- **Uniform,** all units of currency have the same value.

Using money and credit as a lever of change to move to a just economic system assumes these fundamentals as a given. Applied properly, the right form of money can provide the financing for working models demonstrating democratized money power and universal access to capital ownership. To achieve this goal, we would want new money backed by productive assets, and no-interest (but not "no-cost") credit to be channeled to productive business projects in ways that create new owners of the new capital being financed.

The power of money and credit as a lever for change is illustrated by what happened when adequate money and credit became available for industry, agriculture, and commerce. When commercial banking was reinvented during the Renaissance and central banking was invented with the establishment of the Bank of England in 1694,[5] economic development accelerated enormously, as can be seen in the following chart:

The Development Curve

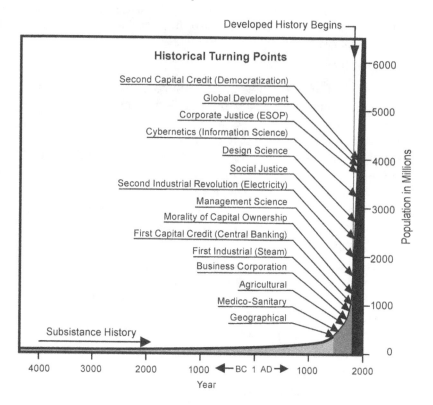

In the United States, the introduction of the leveraged Employee Stock Ownership Plan (ESOP) in the 1950s demonstrated the power of capital credit. When repayable with future corporate profits, capital credit can turn non-owning workers into owners without harming the rights of existing owners.[6]

---

[5] Contrary to popular belief, the Bank of England was not originally established to act as the British government's banker, but to provide "accommodation" (*i.e.*, adequate money, credit, and reserves) to member commercial banks.
[6] Mid South Building Supply, Inc., in Springfield, Virginia, U.S.A., the world's first 100% bank-financed buyout by all the workers, is a successful example of universal capital ownership financing. A similar method of purchasing capital on credit

Tax Policy

In 1891, Pope Leo XIII declared that "Many excellent results will follow" from expanding ownership to as many people as possible.[7] As he said,

[F]irst of all, property will certainly become more equitably divided. . . . . A further consequence will result in the great abundance of the fruits of the earth. Men always work harder and more readily when they work on that which belongs to them; . . . And a third advantage would spring from this: men would cling to the country in which they were born, for no one would exchange his country for a foreign land if his own afforded him the means of living a decent and happy life.[8]

Solving the wealth gap, poverty, and immigration with the same program is surely a desirable outcome. Leo, however, reminded us that,

. . . [t]hese three important benefits, however, can be reckoned on only provided that a man's means be not drained and exhausted by excessive taxation. The right to possess private property is derived from nature, not from man; and the State has the right to control its use in the interests of the public good alone, but by no means to absorb it altogether. The State would therefore be unjust and cruel if under the name of taxation it were to deprive the private owner of more than is fair.[9]

It is not enough, however, merely to say that taxation should not be "unjust and cruel." In order to be practical — for social justice must always be effective — tax policies must reflect and be consistent with the goal of turning as many people as possible into capital owners.

There must, therefore, be legislative initiatives introduced to encourage businesses to finance their growth and expansion in ways that also grow and expand the base of capital ownership in an economy. Tax policy must make it possible for those who own little or no

repayable with future pre-tax corporate profits could be extended to every child, woman and man. Under CESJ's proposed "Economic Democracy Act," no-interest (but not "no-cost") loans would be made, with the right to borrow to purchase qualified investments (e.g., newly issued, voting, full dividend payout shares) allocated equally to each citizen through local commercial banks. Instead of traditional collateral or the seller's loan guarantee as used at Mid South, loans would be secured with private sector capital credit insurance and reinsurance. See CESJ, "Universalizing Capital Ownership: How Article 17 of the Universal Declaration of Human Rights Can Save the Economy," https://www.cesj.org/just-third-way-feature/universalizing-capital-ownership-how-article-17-of-the-universal-declaration-of-human-rights-can-save-the-economy/, accessed May 8, 2020.

[7] *Rerum Novarum*, § 47.

[8] *Ibid.*

[9] *Ibid.*

capital to use pre-tax (*i.e.*, tax-deferred) future savings to accumulate a significant amount of capital in as short a time as possible.

To avoid disrupting an entire economy by introducing a new system all at once, an industry or region could be used as a test case. Once the test case has proved the concept and demonstrated its desirability for the whole economy — accelerated non-inflationary economic growth, expanded purchasing power, increased government revenues from a restored tax base consisting of new capital owners — there could be an overhaul of the tax system as a whole to support and maintain the State and the common good.

Louis Kelso's Employee Stock Ownership Plan (ESOP) illustrates the power of just tax reform. Prior to the tax advantages enacted in the mid-1970s, there were relatively few ESOPs. Once, however, dividends from future profits became tax-deductible at the corporate level if paid through an ESOP, and lenders could exclude from taxable income a certain amount of interest earned, the number of ESOPs increased dramatically. Today in the United States thousands of companies with millions of employees have become worker-owned whole or in part.

Technology

For centuries workers have understood that when technology advances it usually means they will lose their jobs to machines that can do the work better and cheaper. Sometimes advancing technology creates more new jobs than it displaces, although this is not always a benefit. The cotton gin created an enormous demand for labor that was filled by expanding the number of human beings owned as slaves. The Industrial Revolution largely eliminated most production by small and family owned enterprises and turned millions of people into "employees" dependent on private employers and the State.

In the age of robotics and automation, as the rate of technological advancement accelerates, the rate of job creation slows. Finally a point is reached at which the number of jobs eliminated by technology exceeds that of new jobs created.

Of particular importance in this respect are the technological advances in any of the key sectors of the economy, especially energy, agriculture, and robotics. Financed in traditional ways, the ownership of new technologies becomes concentrated. This undermines the ability of most people to gain a living income through their labor or from future capital ownership opportunities.

Financed in ways that allow everyone to have an equal opportunity and means to become an owner of them, the new technologies would shift from having a disruptive effect on the social order to being capable of benefitting every person. Technological advances would no longer be seen as a threat to ordinary people, but as serving their pursuit of a better life.

Abraham Lincoln's 1862 Homestead Act illustrates the importance of widespread capital ownership. In the nineteenth century, a growing number of people were cut off from ownership of technology. This ensured that a combination of the English and European type of liberal democracy (individualist and collectivist, respectively) would emerge in the United States in the twentieth century.

That this should happen in America, "the last, best hope of Earth," was a disaster. Not by coincidence, it could be traced to the failure to maintain an ownership society so that economic democracy could continue to support political democracy. Only the Homestead Act slowed the drift into the Welfare/Servile State, and then only until the available land was taken.

To extend Lincoln's Homestead Act to a technologically advanced economy and restore the institutions of American liberal democracy, we propose an "Economic Democracy Act" (formerly "Capital Homestead Act"). The idea is that instead of being limited to land (which is finite), an Economic Democracy Act would include all forms of productive capital, with particular emphasis on the infinite frontier of advancing technology.

The concept is simple, and could be applied in any society in which productive activity takes place. Specific details, such as required legislation, money and tax reforms, and so on, would have to be tailored to fit particular circumstances and cultures.[10]

In general, however, people without capital would have equal access to no-interest (but not no-cost) commercial bank loans to purchase capital shares to be repaid with the full stream of future profits, with the new money only created to purchase specific capital, and the loan collateralized with capital credit insurance. As the new capital assets generate profits, the loan would be repaid with the future pretax stream of future profits, thereafter providing the new capital owners with a stream of dividend income.

---

[10] See Norman G. Kurland, Dawn K. Brohawn, and Michael D. Greaney, *Capital Homesteading for Every Citizen: A Just Free Market Solution for Saving Social Security*. Arlington, Virginia: Economic Justice Media, 2004.

By empowering every citizen with capital ownership (not just private-sector workers as with the ESOP[11]) and protecting the private property rights of all owners, democratic economic control and thereby political control would be restored to every person. This would gradually reverse today's concentration of economic and political power in the hands of the relatively few who own capital. It would also spread future ownership and power to every citizen, without violating property rights of existing capital owners.

In addition, technological solutions are being developed to address the environmental crisis facing every nation, every human being, and all life on our planet. With expanded access to sound financing, more green technologies, renewable energy systems, and processes for more efficient, non-polluting use of natural resources can be developed and commercialized.

Given these levers of change — Education, Politics, Money and Credit, Tax Policy, and Technology — our social environment can be brought into closer conformity with human nature, that is, with the natural law. This would lay the foundation for a personalist society that promotes the full dignity and development of every human being.

---

[11] *E.g.*, teachers, fire fighters, law enforcement, military, government workers, as well as those who are unable to work, such as children, the disabled, and the elderly.

Closing Comments

Pope Francis faces many challenges in applying Catholic social doctrine to solving today's problems such as the growing wealth, income and power gap in every nation; widespread poverty; destruction of the environment; conflict-driven immigration; growth of State power; the decay of families, and many others.

In particular, Francis is concerned with outreach to the young and others who have been alienated by a Church that seems to have ignored them or passed them by. His greatest challenge, however, may be overcoming a prevailing ignorance or misunderstanding of the principles of personalism and economic personalism. Especially critical is promoting understanding of private property as a fundamental human right, and how universal and equal access to future capital ownership opportunities would make possible lasting, systemic solutions to these problems.

The reason the popes have made private property in capital the centerpiece of Catholic social doctrine is that a person's "social identity" — and thus dignity — depends on having power, and power follows property. As Fulton Sheen noted in his 1940 book, *Freedom Under God*, "Because the ownership of external things is the sign of freedom, the Church has made the wide distribution of private property the cornerstone of her social program."[1]

And what are the results of "freedom under God" achieved through widespread capital ownership? As Pope Leo XIII declared in 1891,

> Many excellent results will follow from this; and, first of all, property will certainly become more equitably divided. . . . If working people can be encouraged to look forward to obtaining a share in the land, the consequence will be that the gulf between vast wealth and sheer poverty will be bridged over, and the respective classes will be brought nearer to one another. A further consequence will result in the great abundance of the fruits of the earth. Men always work harder and more readily when they work on that which belongs to them; nay, they learn to love the very soil that yields in response to the labor of their hands, not only food to eat, but an abundance of good things for themselves and those that are dear to them. That such a spirit of willing labor would add to the produce of the earth and to the wealth of the community is self-evident. And a third advantage would spring from

---

[1] Fulton J. Sheen, *Freedom Under God*. Arlington, Virginia: Economic Justice Media, 2013, 33.

this: men would cling to the country in which they were born, for no one would exchange his country for a foreign land if his own afforded him the means of living a decent and happy life. These three important benefits, however, can be reckoned on only provided that a man's means be not drained and exhausted by excessive taxation. The right to possess private property is derived from nature, not from man; and the State has the right to control its use in the interests of the public good alone, but by no means to absorb it altogether. The State would therefore be unjust and cruel if under the name of taxation it were to deprive the private owner of more than is fair.[2]

As far as Leo XIII was concerned, then, a program like an Economic Democracy Act would provide solutions to most of the problems Francis faces:

- **The Wealth and Income Gap.** "[T]he gulf between vast wealth and sheer poverty will be bridged over, and the respective classes will be brought nearer to one another."
- **Widespread Poverty.** "[This] will result in the great abundance of the fruits of the earth."
- **Destruction of the Environment.** "Men always work harder and more readily when they work on that which belongs to them; nay, they learn to love the very soil that yields in response to the labor of their hands."
- **Conflict-Driven Immigration.** "[M]en would cling to the country in which they were born, for no one would exchange his country for a foreign land if his own afforded him the means of living a decent and happy life."
- **Excessive State Power and the Decay of Families.** "The right to possess private property is derived from nature, not from man; and the State has the right to control its use in the interests of the public good alone, but by no means to absorb it altogether. The State would therefore be unjust and cruel if under the name of taxation it were to deprive the private owner of more than is fair."

The empowering message of the Just Third Way of economic personalism, accompanied by the realistic possibilities for enabling every person to become an economically liberated owner of capital, could assist Pope Francis in his outreach to the young who face a darkening future, and to others who have been alienated by a Church that seems unresponsive to their needs. Demonstrating that the Church presents moral, clear, practical, and relevant guidelines for living what

---

[2] *Rerum Novarum*, § 47.

Aristotle called "the good life" of virtue, may convince many who feel they have been driven out or ignored to return.

Thus, as we discovered in writing this book, there is both a widespread misunderstanding of Catholic social teaching, and a great need for clarification of what is meant by economic justice, and personalism. This has become critical as it relates to the dignity and empowerment of each person within the globalized and high-tech economies of the twenty-first century. It would therefore be appropriate and timely, we believe, for Pope Francis to issue an encyclical to explain economic personalism and teach the principles of economic justice.

Such an encyclical would help guide people everywhere in the challenge of redesigning their basic economic policies and institutions — especially monetary, financial, and tax systems that are today widening the gap between the richest few and the majority of humanity. The goal would be to extend universal and equal capital ownership opportunities in the future without harming property rights of existing owners — to lift up the 99% without pulling down the 1%.

The primary focus of such an encyclical would be the economic empowerment and full development of every person based on the three principles of economic justice: 1) participative justice, 2) distributive justice, and 3) social justice. To clarify further, the encyclical might explain fundamental principles of natural law, the difference between principle (doctrine) and application of principle (discipline), and the reconciliation of individual ethics and social ethics by means of the act of social justice. Ultimately, the goal of such an encyclical would be to persuade people that economic personalism, once understood and applied, has the potential to make the world work for the benefit of everyone.

Such an encyclical could be followed up with an interfaith conference, and then by a series of interdisciplinary conferences, that explore how best to implement economic personalism throughout the world. Religious and spiritual leaders, scholars, policymakers, business people, bankers, labor leaders, environmentalists, social activists, and young people would examine and discuss the personalist principles for reforming the global financial system and establishing just and inclusive market economies.

The goal would be to provide every child, woman, and man in the world with equal access to the means to become capital owners. In this way Pope Francis, as a global teacher, communicator and servant-leader, could catalyze unified action to build a Culture of Life that respects the dignity, empowerment and freedom of every human being.

Questions for Discussion

These are suggested questions and topics for discussion that may also help guide the reader in getting the most out of this book.

Chapter 1: The Question of the Person

1. Why is fideism, deriving truth from faith alone without reference to reason, inadequate as the basis of a religion or a philosophy?
2. What is a person, and why is it important that every human being is automatically a natural person?
3. What are the three basic forms of liberal democracy, and how do they differ from one another?
4. What is the theory of certitude, and why is it important?

Chapter 2: Something Missing

1. What were the two key doctrines defined at the First Vatican Council, and what do they mean?
2. Although *Rerum Novarum* in 1891 was not the first social encyclical, what made it different from earlier social encyclicals?
3. How does the socialist understanding of distributive justice differ from the classical understanding of the virtue?
4. What is Msgr. Taparelli's principle of social justice, and how does it differ from the socialist concept?
5. What is the act of social justice, and how does it permit direct access to the common good?
6. How does solidarity differ from socialism?
7. What are the two types of savings, and what type would allow everyone to participate in capital ownership? How can people without existing savings purchase capital?

Chapter 3: A Theory of Human Dignity

1. What are the five characteristics of Thomist personalism and how are they defined?
2. What distinguishes persons from things, and why is this distinction important?
3. How does the gift of self relate to social charity and social justice?

Chapter 4: Seeking the Good

1. What defines people as human beings, and how does this relate to what is good?
2. What is virtue?

3. What is the common good and why is it essential for human happiness?

Chapter 5: The Political Animal

1. What is collectivism, and why is it not consistent with human dignity?
2. What is individualism, and why is it not consistent with human dignity?
3. What is personalism, and why is it consistent with human dignity?

Chapter 6: Sacred and Inviolable

1. What is private property?
2. Why is private property important for individual human dignity?
3. Why is private property important for a just social order?

Chapter 7: The Economics of Reality and Justice

1. What are the two factors of production in binary economics, and why did Louis Kelso specify only two?
2. Of the five points Hilaire Belloc identified as essential to the restoration of property, he considered money and credit the least important. Louis Kelso considered them the most important. Why and how did Belloc and Kelso differ on this point?
3. How do the Currency Principle and the Banking Principle differ?

Chapter 8: Three Principles of Economic Justice

1. What are the three principles of economic justice?
2. What are the input and output principles, and how do they relate to each other?
3. What is the feedback principle and how does it relate to the input and output principles?

Chapter 9: Four Policy Pillars

1. What are the "Four Policy Pillars of an Economically Just Society"?
2. Why is a free market essential to a personalist society?
3. What is the "fatal omission" from every economy in the world today?

Chapter 10: Five Levers of Change

1. What are the five levers of change?
2. Which lever of change corresponds to the act of social charity?
3. What does it mean to say that human beings are "political animals," and why is this important in understanding social justice?

Selected Bibliography and Resource Guide

Items listed in this bibliography have been limited to those specifically cited in the text and that are readily available. Categorization is somewhat loose, as much of the material fits into more than one category. Labels should be taken as general guidelines.

Church Documents

Mirari Vos (1832)

Singulari Nos (1834)

Quanto Conficiamur (1863)

Rerum Novarum (1891)

Quas Primas (1925)

Quadragesimo Anno (1931)

Divini Redemptoris (1937)

Humani Generis (1950)

Laborem Exercens (1981)

Solicitudo Rei Socialis (1987)

Centesimus Annus (1991)

Catechism of the Catholic Church (1993)

Gratissimam Sane (1994)

Evangelium Vitae (1995)

Ut Unum Sint (1995)

Compendium of the Social Doctrine of the Church (2004)

Caritas in Veritate (2009)

Articles

Alexander, Leo, "Medical Science under Dictatorship," *New England Journal of Medicine*. 1949 July 14; 241 (2): 39–47.

CESJ, "Universalizing Capital Ownership: How Article 17 of the Universal Declaration of Human Rights Can Save the Economy," occasional paper, April 2020.

Greaney, Michael D., "Pope Francis and the Just Third Way," *Homiletic and Pastoral Review*, June 13, 2015.

Kelso, Louis O., "Karl Marx: The Almost Capitalist," *American Bar Association Journal*, March 1957.

Kurland, Norman G., "A New Look at Prices and Money: The Kelsonian Binary Model for Achieving Rapid Growth Without Inflation," *The Journal of Socio-Economics*, 30 (2001) 495-515.

Turner, Frederick Jackson, "The Significance of the Frontier in American History," *Annual Report of the American Historical Association for the Year 1893*. Washington, DC: Government Printing Office, 1894.

Vogüé, Vicomte Eugène Melchior de, "The Neo-Christian Movement in France," *Harper's New Monthly Magazine*, Vol. 84, No. 500, January 1892, 234-242.

Williams, Thomas D., L.C., "What is Thomistic Personalism?" *Alpha Omega*, Vol. VII, No. 2, 2004.

Books — Philosophy and Theology

Adler, Mortimer J., *Ten Philosophical Mistakes: Basic Errors in Modern Thought — How They Came About, Their Consequences, and How to Avoid Them.* New York: Macmillan Publishing Company, 1985.

Adler, Mortimer J., *Truth in Religion: The Plurality of Religions and the Unity of Truth.* New York: Macmillan Publishing Company, 1990.

Adler, Mortimer J., *Adler's Philosophical Dictionary.* New York: Scribner, 1995.

Aquinas, Thomas, *Commentary on Aristotle's Nichomachean Ethics.* Notre Dame, Indiana: Dumb Ox Books, 1993.

Aquinas, Thomas, *Commentary on Aristotle's Politics.* Indianapolis, Indiana: Hackett Publishing Company, Inc., 2007.

Aristotle, *Nichomachean Ethics.* Buffalo, New York: Prometheus Books, 1987.

Aristotle, *Politics.* London: Penguin Books, 1981.

Bocheński, Józef Maria, O.P., *The Methods of Contemporary Thought.* New York: Harper & Row, Publishers, 1968.

Burrow, Jr., Rufus, *God and Human Dignity.* Notre Dame, Indiana: University of Notre Dame Press, 2006.

Chesterton, G.K., *Saint Thomas Aquinas: The "Dumb Ox".* New York: Image Books, 1956.

Knox, Ronald A., *Enthusiasm: A Chapter in the History of Religion with Special Reference to the Seventeenth and Eighteenth Centuries.* New York: Oxford University Press, 1961.

Newman, John Henry, *The Idea of a University.* New Haven, Connecticut: Yale University Press, 1996.

Ratzinger, Joseph, *Europe: Today and Tomorrow.* San Francisco, California: Ignatius Press, 2004.

Ratzinger, Joseph and Pera, Marcello, *Without Roots: The West, Relativism, Christianity, Islam.* New York: Basic Books, 2006.

Sheen, Fulton J., *God and Intelligence in Modern Philosophy.* New York: IVE Press, 2009.

Sheen, Fulton J., *Freedom Under God.* Arlington, Virginia: Economic Justice Media, 2013.

Books — Law, Political Science, and Economics

Bellarmine, Robert, *De Laicis, or, The Treatise on Civil Government.* New York: Fordham University Press, 1928.

Belloc, Hilaire, *An Essay on the Restoration of Property.* New York: Sheed and Ward, 1936.

Belloc, Hilaire, *The Servile State.* Indianapolis, Indiana: Liberty Fund, Inc., 1977.

Briefs, Goetz A., *The Proletariat: A Challenge to Western Civilization*. New York: McGraw-Hill Book Company, 1937.

Crosskey, William W., *Politics and the Constitution in the History of the United States*. Chicago, Illinois: University of Chicago Press, 1953.

Dicey, Albert Venn, *Lectures on the Relation Between Law and Public Opinion in England During the Nineteenth Century*. New Brunswick, New Jersey: Transaction Books, 1981.

Hohfeld, Wesley Newcomb, *Fundamental Legal Conceptions as Applied in Judicial Reasoning*. New Haven, Connecticut: Yale University Press, 1946.

Moulton, Harold G., *The Formation of Capital*. Washington, DC: The Brookings Institution, 1935.

Moulton, Harold G., *The Recovery Problem in the United States*. Washington, DC: The Brookings Institution, 1936.

Moulton, Harold G., *The New Philosophy of Public Debt*. Washington, DC: The Brookings Institution, 1943.

Mueller, Franz H., *The Church and the Social Question*. Washington, DC: American Enterprise Institute for Policy Research, 1984.

Rager, John Clement, *The Political Philosophy of St. Robert Bellarmine*. Spokane, Washington: The Apostolate of Our Lady of Siluva, 1995.

Rommen, Heinrich A., *The Natural Law: A Study in Legal and Social History and Philosophy*. Indianapolis, Indiana: Liberty Fund, Inc., 1998.

Rommen, Heinrich A., *The State in Catholic Thought: A Treatise in Political Philosophy*. St. Louis, Missouri: B. Herder Book Co., 1947.

Sabine, George H., *A History of Political Theory, Third Edition*. New York: Holt, Rinehart and Winston, 1961.

Say, Jean-Baptiste, *Letters to Malthus*. London: Sherwood, Neely, and Jones, 1821.

Sidney, Algernon, *Discourses Concerning Government*. Indianapolis, Indiana: Liberty Fund, Inc., 1996.

Tocqueville, Alexis de, *Democracy in America*. New York: Alfred A. Knoph, Inc., 1994.

Tocqueville, Alexis de, *The Recollections of Alexis de Tocqueville*. Cleveland, Ohio: The World Publishing Company, 1959.

Wooten, David, ed., *Divine Right and Democracy: An Anthology of Political Writings in Stuart England*. London: Penguin Books, 1986.

Books — Economic Personalism and the Just Third Way

Ashford, Robert H.A., and Shakespeare, Rodney, *Binary Economics: The New Paradigm*. Lanham, Maryland: University Press of America, 1999.

Ferree, William J., S.M., Ph.D., *Introduction to Social Justice*. New York: The Paulist Press, 1948.

Ferree, William J., S.M., Ph.D., *The Act of Social Justice*. Washington, DC: The Catholic University of America Press, 1942 (© 1943).

Habiger, Rev. Matthew, O.S.B., Ph.D., *Papal Teachings on Private Property, 1891-1981*. Lanham, Maryland: University Press of America, 1990.

Kelso, Louis O. and Adler, Mortimer J., *The Capitalist Manifesto*. New York: Random House, 1958.

Kelso, Louis O. and Adler, Mortimer J., *The New Capitalists: A Proposal to Free Economic Growth from the Slavery of Savings*. New York: Random House, 1961.

Kelso, Louis O. and Hetter, Patricia, *Two-Factor Theory: The Economics of Reality*. New York: Random House, 1967.

Kurland, Norman G., Brohawn, Dawn K., Greaney, Michael D., *Capital Homesteading for Every Citizen: A Just Free Market Solution for Saving Social Security*. Arlington, Virginia: Economic Justice Media, 2004.

Miller, Rev. John H., S.T.D., *Curing World Poverty: The New Role of Property*. St. Louis, Missouri: Social Justice Review, 1994.

Other Resources

The Center for Economic and Social Justice
https://www.cesj.org

The Just Third Way Blog
http://just3rdwayblogspot.com

Index

About the Authors

Michael D. Greaney. With a degree in Accounting from the University of Notre Dame and MBA from the University of Evansville, Indiana, Michael D. Greaney is Director of Research for the interfaith Center for Economic and Social Justice in Arlington, Virginia. In that capacity he participated in the presentation of a seminar at the Vatican hosted by Achille Cardinal Silvestrini on the importance of widespread capital ownership in combatting global poverty, and co-edited the compendium, *Curing World Poverty: The New Role of Property* (1994). He has appeared on the Eternal Word Television Network's *EWTN Live* with Father Mitch Pacwa. Mr. Greaney lives in Falls Church, Virginia. He is a member of the Ancient Order of Hibernians, Colonel John Fitzgerald Division No. 1, Arlington County, Virginia, and American Mensa, Ltd. He sings with the Washington Men's Camerata and the Saint Thomas More Cathedral Choir. *Economic Personalism: Property, Power and Justice for Every Person* is his sixth book for CESJ.

Dawn K. Brohawn. An expanded ownership education consultant, Dawn Brohawn serves on the Executive Committee of the all-volunteer Center for Economic and Social Justice, which she co-founded in 1984. As CESJ's Director of Communications and chief editor, she has written articles and organized forums on the Just Third Way, Capital Homesteading, and Justice-Based Management[SM]. With Norman Kurland and Michael Greaney, she co-authored *Capital Homesteading for Every Citizen* (2005). She edited *Every Worker an Owner* (1987), the orientation book for President Reagan's Task Force on Project Economic Justice, CESJ's first economic reform initiative. On The ESOP Association's Ownership Culture Committee for seven years, she edited *Journey to an Ownership Culture*, TEA's compendium on model employee-owned companies. Ms. Brohawn co-founded and manages CESJ's Justice University and global Internship and Fellowship Programs.